THE
PORT
HURON
STATEMENT

THE
PORT HURON STATEMENT

The Visionary Call of the 1960s Revolution

TOM HAYDEN

THUNDER'S MOUTH PRESS

NEW YORK

THE PORT HURON STATEMENT
THE VISIONARY CALL OF THE 1960s REVOLUTION

Published by
Thunder's Mouth Press
An Imprint of Avalon Publishing Group Inc.
245 West 17th St., 11th Floor
New York, NY 10011

AVALON
publishing group incorporated

Introduction copyright © 2005 by Tom Hayden
All photos © Tom Hayden unless otherwise credited

First printing September 2005

First published by Students for a Democratic Society
the student Department of the League for Industrial Democracy
New York, 1962

Library of Congress Cataloging-in-Publication Data is available.

ISBN 1-56025-741-5

9 8 7 6 5 4 3 2 1

Book design by Jamie McNeely
Printed in Canada
Distributed by Publishers Group West

CONTENTS

THE
PORT
HURON
STATEMENT

THE WAY WE WERE
AND THE FUTURE OF THE
PORT HURON STATEMENT

OUTSIDE OF PORT HURON, MICHIGAN, WHERE A DENSE thicket meets the lapping shores of Lake Huron, the careful explorer will come across rusty and timeworn pipes and a few collapsed foundations, the last traces of the labor camp where sixty young people finalized the *Port Huron Statement*—the seminal "agenda for a generation"—in 1962.

Some hope that our legacy will be washed out with the refuse in those pipes. Out of sight, out of mind. For the conservative icon Robert Bork, the *Port Huron Statement* (PHS) was considered "a document of ominous mood and aspiration," because of his fixed certainty that, by misreading human nature, utopian movements turn out badly. David Horowitz, a former sixties radical who turned to the hardcore right, dismisses the *PHS* as a "self-conscious effort to rescue the communist project from its Soviet fate." Another ex-leftist, Christopher Hitchens, sees in its pages a conservative reaction to "bigness and anonymity and urbanization," even linking its vision to the Unabomber![1] More progressive writers, such as Garry Wills, E. J. Dionne, and Paul Berman, see the *PHS* as a bright moment of reformist vision that withered due to the impatience and extremism of the young. Excerpts of the *PHS* have been published in countless textbooks, and an Internet search returns numerous references to "participatory democracy," its central philosophic theme. Grassroots movements in Argentina and Venezuela today use "participatory democracy" to describe their popular assemblies and factory takeovers. The historian Thomas Cahill writes that the Greek *ekklesia* was "the world's first participatory democracy" and the model for the early Catholic Church, which "permitted no restrictions on participation: no citizens and non-citizens, no Greeks and non-Greeks, no patriarchs and submissive females."[2] In modern popular culture, authorship of the *PHS* has been claimed by the stoned hippie character played by Jeff Bridges in *The Big Lebowski*.

The story of the 1962 Port Huron convention has been told many times by participants and later researchers, and I will describe it here only briefly so as to focus more on the meaning of the statement itself.[3] The sixty or so young people who met in Port Huron were typically active in the fledgling civil rights, campus reform, and peace movements of the era. Some, like myself, were campus journalists, while others were active in student governments. Some walked picket lines in solidarity with the southern student sit-in movement. More than a few were moved by their religious traditions. My adolescent ambition was to become a foreign correspondent, which was a metaphor for breaking out of the suffocating apathy of the times. Instead, I found myself interviewing and reflecting on southern black dispossessed sharecroppers; students who were willing to go to jail, even die, for their cause; civil rights leader Dr. Martin Luther King Jr. as he marched outside my first Democratic convention; and candidate John Kennedy, giving his speech proposing the Peace Corps on a rainy night in Ann Arbor. I was thrilled by the times in which I lived, and I chose to help build a new student organization, the Students for a Democratic Society, rather than pursue journalism. My parents were stunned.

SDS was the fragile brainchild of Alan Haber, an Ann Arbor graduate student whose father had been a labor official during the last progressive American administration, that of President Franklin Delano Roosevelt. Al was a living link with the fading legacy of the radical left movements that had built the labor movement and the New Deal. He sensed a new spirit among students in 1960 and recruited me to become a "field secretary," which meant moving to Atlanta with my wife, Casey, who had been a leader of the campus sit-ins in Austin, Texas. While participating in the direct action movement and mobilizing national support by writing and speaking on campuses, I learned that passionate advocacy, arising from personal experience, could be a powerful weapon.

Haber and other student leaders across the United States became increasingly aware of a need to connect all the issues that weighed on our generation—apathy, *in loco parentis*, civil rights, the Cold War, the atomic bomb. And so, in December 1961, at twenty-two years of age and fresh from jail as a Freedom Rider in Albany, Georgia, I was asked to begin drafting a document that would express the vision underlying our action. It was to be a short manifesto, a recruiting tool, perhaps five or ten single-spaced pages. Instead it mushroomed into a fifty-page, single-spaced draft prepared for the Port Huron convention in May 1962. That version was debated and rewritten, section by section, by those who attended the five-day Port Huron meeting and was then returned to me for final polishing. Twenty thousand copies were mimeographed and sold for thirty-five cents each.

The vision grew from a concrete generational experience. Rarely, if ever, had students thought of themselves as a force in history or, as we phrased it, an "agency of social change." We were rebelling against the experience of apathy, not against a single specific oppression. We were moved by the heroic example of the black youth in the South, whose rebellion taught us the fundamental importance of race. We were treated legally as wards under our universities' paternal care and could not vote, but as young men we could be conscripted to fight in places we dimly understood, such as Vietnam and Laos. The nation's priorities were frozen by the Cold War: a permanent nuclear arms race benefiting what President Eisenhower had called "the military-industrial complex," whose appetite absorbed the resources we believed were necessary to address the crises of civil rights and poverty, or what John Kenneth Galbraith termed "squalor in the midst of affluence."

Apathy, we came to suspect, was what the administrators and power technicians actually desired. Apathy was not our fault, not an accident, but rather the result of social engineering by those who ran the institutions that taught us, employed us, entertained us, drafted us, bored us, controlled us, wanted us to accept the absolute impossibility of another way of being. It was for this reason that our rhetoric emphasized "ordinary people" developing "out of apathy" (the term was C. Wright Mills's) in order to "make history."[4] Since many of us had emerged from apathetic lives (neither of my parents were political in any sense, and I had attended conservative Catholic schools), we began with the realization that we had to relate to, not denounce, the everyday lives of students and communities around us in order to replicate the journey out of apathy on a massive scale.

We chose to put "values" forward as the first priority in challenging the conditions of apathy and forging a new politics. Embracing values meant making choices as morally autonomous human beings against a world that advertised in every possible way that there were no choices, that the present was just a warm-up for the future.

THE LASTING LEGACY OF PARTICIPATORY DEMOCRACY

The idea of participatory democracy, therefore, should be understood in its psychic, liberatory dimension, not simply as an alternative concept of government organization. Cynics such as Paul Berman acknowledge that the concept of participatory democracy "survived" the demise of the New Left because it "articulated *the existential drama of moral activism.*" (italics added)[5] The notion (and phrase) was transmitted by a philosophy professor in Ann Arbor, Arnold Kaufman, who attended the Port Huron convention. Its roots were as deep and distant as the Native American tribal traditions of consensus.[6] It arose among the tumultuous rebels of western Massachusetts who drove out the British and established self-governing committees in the prelude to the American Revolution. It was

5

common practice among the Society of Friends and in New England's town meetings. It appeared in Thomas Paine's *Rights of Man* in passages exalting "the mass of sense lying in a dormant state" in oppressed humanity, which could be awakened and "excited to action" through revolution.[7] It was extolled (if not always implemented) by Thomas Jefferson, who wrote that every person should believe himself or herself to be "a participator in the government of affairs, not merely at an election one day in the year, but every day."[8] Perhaps the most compelling advocate of participatory democracy, however, was Henry David Thoreau, the nineteenth-century author of *Civil Disobedience*, who opposed taxation for either slavery or war, and who called on Americans to vote "not with a mere strip of paper but *with your whole life.*" Thoreau's words were often repeated in the early days of the sixties civil rights and antiwar movements.

This heritage of participatory democracy also was transmitted to SDS through the works of the revered philosopher John Dewey, who was a leader of the League for Industrial Democracy (LID), the parent organization of SDS, from 1939 to the early 1950s. Dewey believed that "democracy is more than a form of government; it is primarily a mode of associated living, of conjoint communicated experience." It meant participation in all social institutions, not simply going through the motions of elections, and notably, "the participation of every mature human being in the formation of the values that regulate the living of men together."[9]

Then came the rebel sociologist C. Wright Mills, a descendent of Dewey and prophet of the New Left, who died of a heart attack shortly before the *Port Huron Statement* was produced.

Mills had a profound effect in describing a new stratum of radical democratic intellectuals around the world, weary of the stultifying effects of bureaucracy in both the United States and the Soviet Union. His descriptions of the power elite, the mass society, the "democracy without publics," the apathy that turned so many into "cheerful robots," seemed to explain perfectly the need for democracy from the bottom up. The representative democratic system seemed of limited value as long as so many Americans were disenfranchised structurally and alienated culturally. We believed, based on our own experience, that participation in direct action was a method of psychic empowerment, a fulfillment of human potential, a means of curing alienation, as well as an effective means of mass protest. We believed that "ordinary people should have a voice in the decisions that affect their lives," because it was necessary for their dignity, not simply a blueprint for greater accountability.

Some of the Port Huron language appears to be plagiarized from the Vatican's *Pacem in Terris* (*Peace on Earth*).[10] That would be not entirely accidental, because a spirit of peace and justice was flowing through the most traditional of institutions, including southern black Protestant churches, and soon would flourish as Catholic "liberation theology," a direct form of participatory democracy in Third World peasant communities. This "movement spirit" was present everywhere—not only in religion but in music and the arts as well. We studied the lyrics of Bob Dylan more than we did the texts of Marx and Lenin. Dylan even attended an SDS meeting or two. He had hitchhiked east in search of Woody Guthrie, after all. Though never an activist, he expressed our sensibility exactly when he described mainstream culture as "lame as hell and a big trick," where "there was nobody to check with," and folk music as a "guide into some altered consciousness of reality, some different republic, some liberated republic."[11]

The experience of middle-class alienation drew us to Mills's *White Collar*, Albert Camus's *The Stranger*, or Paul Goodman's *Growing Up Absurd*. Our heady sense of the student movement was validated in Mills's "Letter to the New Left" or *Listen Yankee!* The experience of confronting structural unemployment in the "other America" was illuminated by Michael Harrington and the tradition of Marxism. Liberation theology reinforced the concept of living among the poor. The reawakening of women's consciousness was hinted in Doris Lessing's *The Golden Notebook* (which some of us read back-to-back with Clancy Sigal's *Going Away*) or Simone de Beauvoir's *The Second Sex*. The participatory ethic of direct action—of ending segregation, for example, by actually integrating lunch counters—drew from traditions of anarchism as well. (At a small SDS planning meeting in 1960, Dwight Macdonald gave a keynote speech on "The Relevance of Anarchism."[12]) The ethos of direct action leaped from romantic revolutionary novels like Ignazio Silone's *Bread and Wine*, whose hero, a revolutionary masked as a priest, said it "would be a waste of time to show a people of intimidated slaves a different manner of speaking . . . but perhaps it would be worthwhile to show them a different way of living."[13]

The idea was to challenge elite authority by direct example on the one hand, and on the other to draw "ordinary people," whether apathetic students, sharecroppers, or office workers, into a dawning belief in their own right to participate in decisions. This was the method—call it consciousness-raising—of the Student Nonviolent Coordinating Committee, which influenced SDS, the early women's liberation groups, farm workers' house meetings, and Catholic base communities, eventually spreading to Vietnam veterans' rap groups and other organizations. Participatory democracy was a tactic of movement-building as well as an end itself. And by an insistence on *listening* to "the people" as a basic ethic of participatory democracy, the early movement was able to guarantee its roots in American culture and traditions while avoiding the imported ideologies that infected many elements of the earlier left.

Through participatory democracy we could theorize a concrete, egalitarian transformation of the workplaces of great corporations, urban neighborhoods, the classrooms of college campuses, religious congregations, and the structures of political democracy itself. We believed that representative democracy, while an advance over the divine right of kings or bureaucratic dictatorships, should be replaced or reformed by a greater emphasis on decentralized decision-making, remaking our world from the bottom up.

Some of our pronouncements were absurd or embarrassing, like the notion of "cheap" nuclear power becoming a decentralized source of community-based energy, the declaration that "the International Geophysical Year is a model for continuous further cooperation," or the unquestioned utilization of grating sexist terminology ("men" instead of "human beings") in sweeping affirmations about dignity and equality. We could not completely transcend the times, or even predict the near-term future: the rise of the women's and environmental movements, the war in Vietnam, the political assassinations. The gay community was closeted invisibly among us.[14] The beat poets,

9

such as Jack Kerouac and Allen Ginsberg, had stirred us, but the full-blown counterculture, psychedelic drugs such as LSD and mescaline, the Beatles, and the writings of Herbert Marcuse, were two years away.

Yet through many ups and downs, participatory democracy has spread as an ethic throughout everyday life and has become a persistent challenge to top-down institutions all over the world. It has surfaced in campaigns of the global justice movement, in struggles for workplace and neighborhood empowerment, resistance to the Vietnam War draft, in Paulo Freiere's "pedagogy of the oppressed," in political platforms from Green parties to the Zapatistas, in the independent media, and in grassroots Internet campaigns including that of Howard Dean in 2004. Belief in the new participatory norm has resulted in major, if incomplete, policy triumphs mandating everything from freedom-of-information disclosures to citizen participation requirements in multiple realms of official decision-making. It remains a powerful threat to those in established bureaucracies who fear and suppress what they call "an excess of democracy."[15]

THE PORT HURON STRATEGY OF RADICAL REFORM

If the vision of participatory democracy has continuing relevance, so too does the strategic analysis of radical reform at the heart of the *PHS*. Our critique of the Cold War, and liberals who became anticommunist Cold Warriors, bears close resemblance to the contemporary "war on terror" and its liberal Democratic defenders. The Cold War, like today's war on terror, was the organized framework of dominance over our lives. This world was bipolar, divided into good and evil, allies and enemies. The U.S.-led Cold War alliance included any dictators, mafias, or thieving politicians in the world who declared themselves anticommunist. The Cold War alliance scorned the seventy-plus nonaligned nations as being "soft on communism." The United States and its allies engaged in violence or subversion against any governments that included communist or "pro-communist" participation, even if they were democratically elected, such as Guatemala (1954) or Chile (1970). Domestically, the American communists who had helped build the industrial unions, the Congress of Industrial Organizations, the defense of the Scottsboro Boys, the racial integration of major league baseball, who had joined the war against Hitler, suddenly found themselves purged or blacklisted as "un-American" for the very pro-Soviet sympathies that had been popular during World War II.[16] The parallels with today's war-on-terror coalition (including unstable dictatorships like Pakistan and Uzbekistan), and between the McCarthy-era witch hunts and today's Patriot Act roundups of "suspicious" Muslims, are eerie. Then it was a ubiquitous "atomic spy ring," today it is the omnipresent Al Qaeda. The externalizing of the feared, ubiquitous, secretive, religiously alien, and foreign "communist" or "terrorist" enemy, the drumbeat of fear issuing from "terror alerts" and mass-media sensationalism, the dominance of military spending over any other priority, and the ever-increasing growth of a National Security State—all of these themes of the Cold War have been revived in our country's newest crusade.

Of course the "threat" of violence is not imaginary. Raging militants have attacked innocent Americans and are likely to do so again. Our government's $30 billion intelligence budget failed to stop them. But those who question the current military priorities or dare to speak of root causes—addressing the abject misery and poverty of billions of people that contributed to the growth of communism in the past or Islamic militancy today— are dismissed too often as enemy sympathizers or soft-headed pacifists who cannot be trusted with questions of national security ("sentimentalists, the utopians, the wailers," historian Arthur Schlesinger called them during the Cold War).[17] Today such people are accused of "blaming America first" by critics from neoconservative Jeanne Kirkpatrick to former SDS leader Todd Gitlin.[18] In the Cold War days, the CIA routinely funded a covert class of liberal anticommunists everywhere from the American Committee for Cultural Freedom to the AFL-CIO to the U.S. National Student Association.[19] There is a direct line, even a genealogical one, from the leaders of those groupings, such as Irving Kristol and Norman Podhoretz, to their neoconservative descendants, such as William Kristol, editor of the *Weekly Standard*, and John Podhoretz, and from the forties celebration of "the American Century" to today's neoconservative project, the Project for the New American Century. As for the definition of "the enemy," during the Cold War it was a conspiracy centralized in Moscow through a myriad of puppet regimes and parties; today it is Al Qaeda, an invisible network consolidated and controlled by Osama bin Laden and a handful of conspirators.

The *Port Huron Statement* properly dissociated itself from the Soviet Union and communist ideology, just as antiwar critics today are opposed to Al Qaeda's religious fundamentalism or terror against civilians. But the *PHS* broke all taboos by identifying the Cold War itself as the framework that blocked our aspirations.[20] As a result, SDS was accused of being insufficiently "anticommunist" by some of its patrons in the older liberal left who had been deeply devoted to the liberal anticommunist crusade.[21] The truth lay in contrasting generational experiences: we were inspired by the civil rights movement, by the hope of ending poverty, with the gap between democratic promise and inequality as reality. The Cold War focused our nation's attention and its budget priorities outward on enemies abroad rather than on the enemies in our face at home. The nuclear arms race and permanent war economy drained any resources that could be devoted to ending poverty or hunger, either at home or among the wretched of the earth. Most, not all, of the liberal establishment—the people we had looked up to—left behind their idealistic roots and became allied to the military-industrial complex. Today a similar transition has occurred among many within the Democratic Party's establishment. Despite their roots in civil rights and antipoverty programs, they have become devotees of a corporate agenda, promoting the privatization of public assets from Latin America to the Middle East, creating the undemocratic World Trade Organization, whose rules taken literally would define the New Deal as a "restraint on trade."[22] With the attacks of September 11, 2001, many of the same liberals have abandoned their pasts in the anti-Vietnam movement, or the McCarthy, Kennedy, and McGovern campaigns, to pass the Patriot Act, invade Afghanistan and Iraq, justify the use of torture and detention without trial, and expand the Big Brother national security apparatus, while leaving the United States at the bottom among industrialized countries in its contributions to United Nations programs to combat hunger, illiteracy, and drinking-water pollution.[23] Consistent with the Cold War era, any politician who questions these priorities, even a decorated war veteran, will be castigated as soft on terrorism and effectively threatened with political defeat.[24]

The *Port Huron Statement* called for a coalescing of social movements: civil rights, peace, labor, liberals, and students. It was an original formulation at the time, departing from the centrality of organized labor, or the working class, that had governed the left for decades and it caused some of our elders to grind their teeth. The *PHS* reaffirmed that labor was crucial to any movement for social change, while chastising the labor "movement" for having become "stale." The Port Huron vision was far more populist, more middle-class, more quality-of-life in orientation than the customary platforms of the left. The election of an Irish Catholic president in 1960 symbolized the assumed assimilation of the white ethnics into the middle class and offered hope that people of color would follow in turn. The goal of racial integration was little questioned. Women had not begun to challenge patriarchy. Environmentalism had yet to assault the metaphysic of "growth." And so we could envision unifying nearly everyone around fulfillment of the New Deal dream. The *PHS* connected issues not like a menu, not as gestures to diverse identity movements, but more seamlessly, by declaring that the civil rights, antipoverty, and peace movements could realize their dreams by refocusing America's attention to an unfulfilled domestic agenda instead of the Cold War.

The document contained an explicit electoral strategy as well, envisioning the "realignment" of the Democratic Party into a progressive instrument. The strategy was to undermine the racist "Dixiecrat" element of the party through the southern civil rights movement and its national support network. The

Dixiecrats not only dominated the segregationist political economy of the South but the crucial committees on military spending in the U.S. Congress as well. The racists also were the hawks. By undermining the southern segregationists, we could weaken the institutional supports for greater military spending and violent anticommunism. The party would thus "realign" as white southerners defected to the Republicans, black southerners registered as Democrats, and the national party retained its New Deal liberal leanings. Through realignment, some of us dreamt, a radical-liberal governing coalition could achieve political power in America—in our lifetime, through our work.

This is the challenge that SDS took on: to argue against "unreasoning anticommunism," to demand steps toward arms reductions and disarmament, to channel the trillions spent on weapons toward ending poverty in the world and at home. It was the kind of inspired thinking of which the young are most often capable, but it also was relevant to the times. After Port Huron, Haber and I traveled to the White House to brief Arthur Schlesinger on our work, hoping to spark a dialogue about the new movements. There were a handful of liberal White House staffers like Harris Wofford and Richard Goodwin who seemed to take an interest. We also had funds and the goodwill of Walter Reuther, president of the United Auto Workers (whose top assistant, Mildred Jeffrey, happened to be the mother of Sharon Jeffrey, an Ann Arbor SDS activist).

History has completely ignored, or forgotten, how close we came to implementing this main vision of the *Port Huron Statement*. President John Kennedy and his counterparts in Moscow were considering a historic turn away from the Cold

War arms race, sentiments the president would express quite boldly just before he was killed. At a time when his generals sought a first-strike policy, Kennedy promoted a nuclear test ban treaty and offered a vision beyond the Cold War in August 1963, three months before the assassination. At the same time, Kennedy's positions on civil rights and poverty were rapidly evolving as well. At first the Kennedys had been taken aback by the Freedom Riders, with Attorney General Robert Kennedy wondering aloud if we had "the best interest of the country at heart" or were providing "good propaganda for America's enemies."[25] President Kennedy can be heard on White House tapes calling the Student Nonviolent Coordinating Committee (SNCC) and its chairman, future Congressman John Lewis[26] "sons of bitches."[27] "The problem with you people," Kennedy once snapped, [is that] you want too much too fast."[28] In this sense, the Kennedys were reflecting, not shaping, the mood of the country. Sixty-three percent of Americans opposed the Freedom Rides that preceded Port Huron. The *New York Times* opined that "nonviolence that deliberatively provokes violence is a logical contradiction."[29] President Kennedy, who at first opposed the March on Washington as being too politically provocative, finally changed his mind and instead welcomed the civil rights leadership to the White House.[30] By the time of his assassination, he and his brother Bobby were almost becoming "brothers" in the eyes of the civil rights leadership. In addition to their joint destiny with the civil rights cause, Kennedy was sparking a public interest in attacking poverty, having read and recommended Mike Harrington's *The Other America*. One of the original plans for the War on Poverty, according to a biography of Sargeant Shriver, was "empowering the poor to agitate against the local political structure for institutional reform," which would have aligned the administration closely—perhaps too closely—with SNCC and SDS community organizers.[31]

For Kennedy to truly address poverty and racism in a second term would have required a turn away from the nuclear arms race and the budding U.S. counterinsurgency war in Vietnam. Robert Kennedy suggested as much in a 1964 interview: "For the first few years . . . [JFK] had to concentrate all his energies . . . on foreign affairs. He thought that a good deal more was needed domestically. The major issue was the question of civil rights. . . . Secondly, he thought that we really had to begin to make a major effort to deal with unemployment and the poor in the United States."[32] Despite efforts by today's neoconservatives to portray Kennedy as a Cold War hawk, the preponderance of evidence is that he intended to withdraw all American troops from Vietnam by 1965. Two days before his murder, for example, the administration announced plans to withdraw 1,000–1,300 troops from South Vietnam. But two days after his death, on November 24, a covert plan was adopted in National Security Memorandum 273 that authorized secret operations, "graduated in intensity," against North Vietnam.[33]

The assassination of President John F. Kennedy was the first of several catastrophic murders that changed all our lives; and the trajectory of events imagined at Port Huron was also changed. The dates must be kept in mind: most of us who assembled there were about twenty-one years old in June 1962. An idealistic social movement was exploding, winning attention from a new administration. Just as we had hoped, the March on Washington made race and poverty the central moral issues facing the country; the peace movement would hear a president pledging to end the cold war. But then a murder derailed the new national direction. I was about to turn twenty-four when Kennedy was killed. The experience will forever shadow the meaning of the sixties. The very concept of a presidential assassination was completely outside my youthful expectations for the future. No matter what history may reveal about the murder, the feeling was chillingly inescapable that the sequence of the president's actions on the Cold War and racism soon led to his death. The subsequent assassinations of the Reverend Martin Luther King Jr. and Senator Robert Kennedy in 1968 permanently derailed what remained of the hopes that were born at Port Huron. Whether one believes the murders were conspiracies or isolated accidents, the effect was to destroy the progressive political potential of the sixties and leave us all as "might-have-beens," in the phrase of the late Jack Newfield.

Hope died slowly and painfully. There still was hope in the year following President Kennedy's murder—for example, in the form of the Mississippi Freedom Democratic Party, the most important organized embodiment of the Port Huron hope for political realignment. Organized by SNCC in 1963–1964, the MFDP was a grassroots Democratic Party led by Mississippi's dispossessed blacks, with the goal of seeking recognition from the national Democratic Party at its 1964 convention in Atlantic City. The MFDP originated in November 1963, the very month of the Kennedy assassination, when ninety thousand blacks in Mississippi risked their lives to set up a "freedom vote" to protest their exclusion from the political process. Then came Freedom Summer 1964, including the kidnapping and murders of James Cheney, Andrew Goodman, and Mickey Schwerner. FBI director J. Edgar Hoover at first suggested that the missing activists had staged their own disappearance to inflame tensions, or perhaps that "these three might have gotten rather fresh."[34]

Next, just before the Democratic convention, on August 2, the United States fabricated a provocation in the Gulf of Tonkin that expanded the Vietnam War along the lines suggested in NSM 273 ("a very delicate subject," according to Pentagon chief Robert McNamara[35]). President Johnson drafted his war declaration on August 4, the same day the brutalized bodies of three civil rights workers were found in a Mississippi swamp. On August 9, at a memorial service in a burned-out church, SNCC leaders questioned why the U.S. government was declaring war on Vietnam but not on racism at home. On August 20, Johnson announced the official "War on Poverty" with an appropriation of less than one billion dollars while signing a military appropriation fifty times greater.[36] The War on Poverty—the core of the Port Huron generation's demand for new priorities—was dead on arrival. The theory, held by historian William Appleman Williams among others, that foreign policy crises were exploited to deflect America's priorities away from racial and class tensions, seemed to be vindicated before our eyes.

Johnson was plotting to use the party's leading liberals, many of them sympathetic to the fledgling SDS, to undermine the civil rights challenge from the Mississippi Freedom Democrats three weeks after the Gulf of Tonkin incident. Hubert Humphrey was assigned the task, apparently to test his loyalty to Johnson before being offered the vice presidential slot. He lectured the arriving freedom delegation that the president would "not allow that illiterate woman (the MFDP leader Fannie Lou Hamer) to speak from the floor of the convention."[37] Worse, the activists were battered by one of their foremost icons, the UAW's Walter Reuther, who was flown by private jet to quell the freedom challenge; he told Humphrey and others that "we can reduce the opposition to this to a microscopic fraction so they'll be completely unimportant."[38] White House tape transcripts show clearly that Johnson thought the Freedom Democrats would succeed if the matter was put to a convention vote.

This became a turning point between those who tried bringing their "morality to politics, not politics to their morality," said Bob Moses, then a central figure for both SNCC and SDS. It was so intense that Humphrey broke down and cried. At one point LBJ stole off to bed in the afternoon, spending the next twenty-four hours vowing to quit the presidency.[39] The Mississippi Freedom Democrats and the hopes of the early sixties were crushed once again, this time not by the clubs of southern police but by the hypocrisy of liberalism. If Johnson had incorporated the Mississippi Freedom delegation, we believed, he still could have defeated Barry Goldwater that November and hastened the political realignment we stood for. But the possibility of transformation evaporated. In the resulting vacuum the first Black Panther Party for Self-Defense was born, in Lowndes County, Alabama, in response to the rejection of the MFDP. Only days after the convention, while Johnson was mouthing the words "no wider war," his national security advisor, McGeorge Bundy, was suggesting that "substantial armed forces" would be sent.[40]

That fall, the Port Huron generation of SDS met in New York

to ponder the options. Just two years before, the war in Vietnam seemed so remote that it barely was noted in the *PHS*. Some of us, following the SNCC model and convinced that realignment was under way, had moved to inner cities to begin organizing a broad coalition of the poor, under the name Economic Research and Action Project (ERAP). Others were excited about the Berkeley Free Speech Movement and prospects for campus rebellion. Still others were planning protests if the Vietnam War should escalate. Amid great apprehension, the SDS national council adopted the slogan "Part of the Way with LBJ." While the president vowed never to send America's young men to fight a land war in Southeast Asia, even on election day the White House was nevertheless drafting plans for expanding the war.[41] By springtime, 150,000 young American men were dispatched to war. In May, SDS led the largest antiwar protest in decades in Washington, D.C. But it was too late to stop the machine. Having learned that assassinations could change history, our generation now began to also learn that official lies were packaged as campaign promises.

The utopian period of Port Huron was over, less than three years after the *PHS* was issued. The vision would flicker but would never be recovered amid the time of radicalization and polarization ahead. Since the Democratic Party had failed the MFDP and launched the Vietnam War, those favoring an electoral strategy were frustrated and marginalized. Resistance grew in the form of urban insurrections, GI mutinies, draft card burnings, building takeovers, and bombings. Renewed efforts at reforming the system, such as the 1967–1968 Eugene McCarthy presidential campaign, helped to unseat LBJ but failed to capture the Democratic nomination. RFK was the last politician who had rekindled the hopes of realizing the vision of Port Huron, not only with interest in antipoverty programs and his gradual questioning of Vietnam, but most eloquently with his 1967 speech challenging the worth of the Gross National Product as a measure of well-being. I supported his candidacy, stood over his coffin, and finally embraced the transmutation of hope to rage. After Nixon's election, I was convicted as part of the so-called Chicago Eight of inciting a riot at the 1968 Democratic convention, a judicial process that ended in our acquittal in 1973. By then the long-awaited political realignment was partly under way, starting with Senator George McGovern's 1972 presidential campaign, then leading to the ascension of southern liberals like Jimmy Carter, Bill Clinton, Al Gore, Andrew Young, and John Lewis to national power. But by now it was too late to keep white southerners in the Democratic Party with populist economic promises. The threat to their southern white traditions drove them into the Republican Party. It was Richard Nixon's strategy of realignment that prevailed.[42]

The importance of the mid-sixties turning points, however, are missed by most historians of the era, who tend to blame SDS for "choosing" to become more radical, sectarian, dogmatic, and violent, as if there was no context for the evolution of our behavior. Garry Wills, whose book *Nixon Agonistes* extolled the *Port Huron Statement*,[43] later blamed the young radicals for having prolonged the Vietnam War.[44] In his view, the movement should have practiced constructive nonviolence, as Dr. King promoted, which aimed at gaining national acceptance. This analysis ignores the fact that Dr. King himself was becoming radicalized by 1966, and starting to despair of nonviolence. Liberal bastions like the *New York Times* editorially blasted him for speaking out against the Vietnam War in 1967. His murder and that of Robert Kennedy stoked violent passions among many of the young. Wills also writes that it was easier to unite Americans against the manifest evil of racism than against the Vietnam War, in which, he believes, "the establishment was not so manifestly evil."[45] But for our generation, the fact that the U.S. government dropped more bombs on Vietnam than it did everywhere during World War II, while lying to those it was conscripting, was a manifest evil. Wills writes that the Chicago police simply "lost their heads" in Chicago, as if the beatings and gassings of more than sixty journalists was somehow "provoked." Wills laments that "civil disobedience had degenerated into terrorism,"[46] but does not acknowledge the causes or the fact that violent rebellions were taking place in both the armed forces and American ghettos and barrios at an unprecedented rate. Were the student radicals to blame for this turn toward confrontation, or was it explainable by the failure of an older generation to complete the reforms begun in the early sixties instead of invading Vietnam? As Wills himself wrote in his 1969 book, "the generation gap is largely caused by elders who believe they have escaped it."[47]

Similarly, some still believe that the election of Hubert Humphrey in 1968 would have ended the Vietnam War and restored liberalism as a majority coalition. Who is to say? Humphrey remains an icon for an older generation of liberals to this day. For the Port Huron generation of SDS and SNCC, however, he remains the symbol of how liberalism, driven by opportunism, chose Vietnam over the Mississippi Freedom Democrats. Regardless of which view one chooses, the forgotten fact is that Humphrey probably would have won the

1968 election if he had taken an independent antiwar stand. In late October, Nixon led 44–36 percent. With the election one week away, the United States ordered a bombing halt and offered talks. On November 2 both the Gallup and Harris Polls showed Nixon's lead shaved to 42–40 percent. According to historian Theodore White, "had peace become quite clear, in the last three days of the election of 1968, Hubert Humphrey would have won the election."[48] The final result was Nixon 43.4 percent, Humphrey 42.7 percent—a margin of 0.7 percent. Would Humphrey have ended the war? Perhaps, perhaps not. But there is no single factor that leads to a loss by less than 1 percent. Anyone who magnifies the blame toward one group or another is indulging in self-interested scapegoating.[49]

There is no doubt that by the decade's end many of us, myself certainly included, had evolved from nonviolent direct action to acceptance of self-defense, or street fighting against the police and authorities, or hiding fugitives underground. On the day the Chicago Eight were convicted, for example, there were some several hundred riots in youth communities and college campuses across the country, including the burning of a Bank of America by university students in Isla Vista. No one could have ordered this behavior; it was the spontaneous response of hundreds of thousands of young people to the perceived lack of effectiveness of either politics or nonviolence. As Kirkpatrick Sale notes, a Gallup Poll in the late sixties showed one million university students identifying themselves as "revolutionary."[50] What many fail to ask is where it all began, where the responsibility lay for causing this massive alienation among college students, inner-city residents, and grunts in the U.S. military. It is convenient to blame the teenagers and twenty-somethings in the sixties for "losing their heads," unlike the heavily armed and professionally trained Chicago police who knew their "riot" would be approved by their mayor. "Vietnam undid the New Left," Wills writes, because it "blurred the original aims" of the SDS.[51] One wishes in this case that Wills had dwelt on how Vietnam undid America.

When the period we know as "the sixties" finally ended—from exhaustion, infighting, FBI counterintelligence programs and, most of all, from success in ending the Vietnam War and pushing open doors to the mainstream[52]—I turned my energies increasingly toward electoral politics, serving eighteen years in the California legislature, chairing policy committees on labor, higher education, and the environment. This was not so much a "zigzag" as an effort to act as an outsider on the inside.[53] It was consistent with the original vision of Port Huron, but played itself out during a time of movement decline or exhaustion.

The lessons I learned while in office were contradictory. On the one hand, there was much greater space to serve movement goals on the inside than I had imagined in 1962; one could hold press conferences, hire activist staff, call watchdog hearings with subpoena power, and occasionally pass far-reaching legislation (divestment from South Africa, antisweatshop guidelines, endangered species laws, billions for conservation, etc.). Perhaps the most potent opportunities were insurgent political campaigns themselves, raising new issues in the public arena and politicizing thousands of new activists in each cycle. On the other hand, there was something impenetrable about the system of power as a whole. The state had permanent, neo-Machiavellian interests of its own, deflecting or absorbing any democratic pressures that became too threatening. The state served and brokered a wider constellation of private corporate and professional interests that expected profitable investment opportunities and law and order, when needed, against dissidents, radicals, or the angry underclass. These undemocratic interests could reward or punish politicians through their monopoly of campaign contributions, media campaigns and, ultimately, capital flight. The absence of a multiparty system with solidly progressive electoral districts was another factor in producing compromised and centrist outcomes. I think of those two decades in elected office as an honorable interlude, carrying forward or protecting the gains of one movement while waiting for others to begin, as happened with the antisweatshop and anti-WTO campaigns in the late 1990s.

THE ACHIEVEMENTS OF THE SIXTIES

SDS could not survive the sixties as an organization. In part, the very ethos of participatory democracy conflicted with the goal, shared by some at Port Huron, of building a permanent New Left organization. Not only was there a yearly turnover of the campus population, but SDS activists were committed in principle to leave the organization in two or three years to make room for new leadership. Meanwhile, it seemed that new radical movements were exploding everywhere, straining the capacity of any single organization like SDS to define, much less coordinate, the whole. Administrators, police, and intelligence agencies alternated between strategies of co-optation, counterintelligence, and coercion. SDS disintegrated into rival Marxist sects that had been unimaginable to us in 1962, and those groups devoured the host organization by 1969. (I would argue that one of them, the Weather Underground, was an authentic descendent of the Port Huron generation, rebelling in part against the failure of our perceived reformism.)

But it would be a fundamental mistake to judge the participatory sixties through any organizational history. SDS, following SNCC, was a catalytic organization, not a bureaucratic one. The two groups catalyzed more social change in their seven-year lifespans than many respectable and well-funded nongovernmental organizations accomplish in decades.[54] If anything, the sixties were a triumph for the notions of decentralized democratic movements championed in the *Port Huron Statement*. Slogans like "let the people decide" were heartfelt. The powerful dynamics of the sixties could not have been "harnessed" by any single structure; instead, the heartbeat was expressed through countless innovative grassroots networks that rose or fell based on voluntary initiative. The result was a vast change in public attitudes as the sixties became mainstreamed.

In this perspective the movement outlived its organized forms, such as SDS. Once any organizational process became dysfunctional (national SDS meetings began drawing three thousand participants, for example), the movement energy flowed around the structural blockages, leaving the organizational shell for the squabbling factions. For example, in the very year that SDS collapsed, there were millions in the streets for the Vietnam Moratorium and the first Earth Day. In the first six months of 1969, based on information from only 232 of America's 2,000 campuses, over 200,000 students were involved in protests, 3,652 were arrested, and 956 suspended or expelled. In 1969–1970, according to the FBI, 313 building occupations took place. In Vietnam, there were 209 fraggings (slang for an attack on a superior) by soldiers in

1970 alone. Public opinion had shifted from 61 percent supporting the Vietnam War in 1965 to 61 percent declaring the war was wrong in 1971.[55] The goals of the early SDS were receiving majority support while the organization became too fragmented to benefit.

When a movement declines, no organization can resuscitate it. This is not to reject the crucial importance of organizing, or the organizer's mentality, or the construction of a "civil society" of countless networks. But it is to suggest a key difference between movements and institutions. The measure of an era is not taken in membership cards or election results alone, but in the changes in consciousness, in the changing norms of everyday life, and in the public policies that result from movement impacts on the mainstream. Much of what we take for granted—voting by renters, weekends, clean drinking water, the First Amendment, collective bargaining, interracial relationships—is the result of bitter struggles by radical movements of yesteryear to legitimate what previously was considered antisocial or criminal. In this sense, the effects of movements envisioned at Port Huron, and the backlash against them, are deep, ongoing, and still contested.

First of all, American *democracy indeed became more participatory* as a result of the sixties. More constituencies gained a voice and a public role than ever before. The political process became more open. Repressive mechanisms were exposed and curbed. The culture as a whole became more tolerant.

Second, there were structural or institutional *changes that redistributed political access and power.* Jim Crow segregation was ended in the South, and 20 million black people won the vote. The eighteen-year-old vote enfranchised another 10 million young people. Affirmative action for women and people of color broadened opportunities in education, the political process, and the workplace. The opening of presidential primaries empowered millions of voters to choose their candidates. New checks and balances were imposed on an imperial presidency. Two presidents, Lyndon Johnson and Richard Nixon, were forced from office.

Third, *new issues and constituencies were recognized in public policy*: voting rights acts, the Clean Air and Water Acts, the endangered species laws, the Environmental Protection Agency, the Occupational Health and Safety Act, consumer safety laws, nondiscrimination and affirmative action initiatives, the disability rights movement, and others. A rainbow of identity movements, including the American Indian Movement (AIM), the Black Panther Party, and the Young Lords Party, staked out independent identities and broadened the public discourse.

Fourth, *the Vietnam War was ended and the Cold War model was challenged.* Under public pressure, the U.S. Congress eliminated military funding for South Vietnam and Cambodia. The Watergate scandal, which arose from Nixon's repression of antiwar voices, led to a presidential resignation. The United States ended the military draft. The Carter administration provided amnesty for Vietnam-era deserters. Beginning with Vietnam and Chile, human rights was established as an integral part of national security policy. Relations with Vietnam were normalized by President Bill Clinton, a former McCarthy and McGovern activist, Senator John Kerry, a former leader of Vietnam Veterans Against the War (VVAW), and Senator John McCain, a former POW in Hanoi.[56]

Fifth, *the sixties consciousness gave birth to new technologies,* including the personal computer, which led to participatory democracy in global communication. I remember seeing my first computer as a graduate student at the University of Michigan in 1963; it seemed as large as a room, and my faculty adviser, himself a campus radical, promised that all our communications would become radically decentralized with computers the size of my hand. "It is not a coincidence," writes an industry analyst, "that, during the 60's and early 70's, at the height of the protest against the war in Vietnam, the civil rights movement and widespread experimentation with psychedelic drugs, personal computing emerged from a handful of government- and corporate-funded laboratories, as well as from the work of a small group . . . [who] were fans of LSD, draft resisters, commune sympathizers and, to put it bluntly, long-haired hippie freaks."[57] While it is fair to say the dream of technology failed, there is no doubt that the Internet has propelled communication and solidarity among global protest movements like never before, resulting in a more participatory, decentralized democratic process.

The sixties, however, are far from over. Coinciding with their progressive impacts has been a constant and rising backlash to limit, if not roll back, the social, racial, environmental, and political reforms of the era. Former President Clinton, an astute observer of our political culture, says that the sixties remain the basic fault line running through American politics to this day and provide the best measure of whether one is a Democrat or a Republican. It is important to note that the sixties revolt was a global phenomenon, producing a lasting "generation of '68" that shares power in many countries, including Germany, France, Mexico, Brazil, Argentina, Uruguay, Chile, Northern Ireland, South Africa, South Korea, to name only a few.

Social movements begin and end in memory. The fact that we called ourselves a "new" left meant that our radical roots largely had been severed, by McCarthyism and the Cold War, so that the project of building an alternative was commencing all over again. Social movements move from the mysterious margins to the mainstream, become majorities, then are subject to crucial arguments over memory. The sixties are still contested terrain in schools, the media, and politics precisely because the recovery of their meaning is important to social movements of the future and because the suppression or distortion of that memory is vital to the conservative agenda. We are nearing the fiftieth anniversary of every significant development of the sixties, including the *Port Huron Statement*. The final stage of the sixties, the stage of memory and museums, is under way.

STUDENTS, THE UNIVERSITIES, AND THE POSTMODERN LEGACY

Of all the contributions of the *Port Huron Statement*, perhaps the most important was the insight that university communities had a role in social change. Universities had become as indispensable to economics in what we called the automation age as factories were in the age of industrial development. Robert McNamara, after all, was trained at the University of Michigan. In a few years, University of California president Clark Kerr would invent the label "multiversity" to explain the importance of knowledge to power.

Clearly, the CIA understood the importance of universities; as early as 1961, as the *Port Huron Statement* was being conceived, its chief of covert action wrote that books were "the most important weapon of strategic propaganda."[58]

We saw the possibilities, therefore, in challenging or disrupting the role of the universities in the knowledge economy. More important, however, was the alienation that the impersonal mass universities bred among idealistic youth searching for "relevance," as described in some of the most eloquent passages of the *PHS*. We wanted participatory education in our participatory democracy, truth from the bottom up, access to the colleges and universities for those who had historically been excluded. Gradually, this led to a fundamental rejection of the narratives we had been taught, the myths of the American melting pot, the privileged superiority of (white) Western civilization, and inevitably to the quest for inclusion of "the other"—the contributions of women, people of color, and all those who had been marginalized by the march of power. The result of this subversion of traditional authority became known as multiculturalism, deconstruction, and postmodernism. In his perceptive 1968 study, *Young Radicals: Notes on Committed Youth*, Harvard researcher Kenneth Kenniston was among the first to conclude that our "approach to the world—fluid, personalistic, anti-technological, and non-violent—suggests the emergence of what I will call the post-modern style."[59] It could also be called the Port Huron style—the endless improvising, the techniques of dialogue and participation, learning through direct action, the rejection of dogma while searching for theory. It was typical of this style that the *PHS* was offered as a "living document," not a set of marching orders.

When I first met Howard Zinn, he was a professor at a black women's college in Atlanta, where both of us were immersed in the early civil rights movement. He was one of the most deeply-engaged intellectuals I had ever met. While witnessing and participating in the civil rights movement, he was discovering a "story" far different than the conventional one he knew as a trained historian. It eventually was published as *A People's History of the United States*, selling over a million copies, even though Zinn was fired once from Spelman and almost fired from Boston University for promoting civil rights and anti-Vietnam activism.

Thanks to Zinn and numerous subsequent writers, the "disappeared" of history were suddenly appearing in new narratives and publications developed in ethnic studies, women's studies, African American studies, Chicano studies, queer studies, and environmental studies. Films like *Roots, The Color Purple,* and *Taxi Driver* expanded and deepened this discovery process. Conservatives like Lynne Cheney, wife of vice president Dick Cheney, were distressed that more young people knew of Harriett Tubman than the name of the commandeer of the American Revolutionary Army (George Washington).[60]

Cheney has been working since the Reagan era to undercut the sixties cultural revolution, but the effort is not simply Republican. Among the corporate Democrats, Larry Summers, former treasury secretary and now president of Harvard, is devoted to "eradicating the influence of the 1960s," according to a recent biography.[61]

The unexpected student revolt that produced the *Port Huron Statement* was the kind of moment described by the French philosopher of deconstruction, Jacques Derrida, who took the side of the French students at the barricades in 1968. In his words, Derrida tried to "distinguish between what one calls the *future* and '*l'avenir.'* There's a future that is predictable, programmed, scheduled, foreseeable. But there is a future, l'avenir (to come), which refers to someone who comes whose arrival is totally unexpected. For me, that is the real future. That which is totally unpredictable. The Other who comes without my being able to anticipate its arrival. So if there is a real future beyond this other known future, it's l'avenir in that it's the coming of the Other when I am completely unable to foresee its arrival."[62]

The *Port Huron Statement* announced such an unexpected arrival with a simple introductory sentence: "We are people of this generation, bred in at least modest comfort, housed now in universities, looking uncomfortably at the world we inherit." Now as that same Port Huron generation enters into its senior years, it is worth asking whether we are uncomfortable about the world we are passing on as inheritance, and what may still be done. For me, the experience of the sixties will always hold a bittersweet quality, and I remain haunted by another question raised by Ignazio Silone in *Bread and Wine:* "What would happen if men remained loyal to the ideals of their youth?"[63]

Now that deconstruction has succeeded, is it time for reconstruction again? The postmodern cannot be an end state, only a transition to the unexpected future. Transition to what? Not an empire, not a fundamentalist retreat from modernity, for they are not answers to the world crisis. As the *Port Huron Statement* said, "The world is in transition. But America is not." New global peace and justice movements, symbolized by the 1999 Seattle protests against the World Trade Organization, declare that "another world is possible," echoing the Zapatista call for "a world in which all worlds fit." The demands of these new rebels are transitional too, toward a new, inclusive narrative in addition to the many narratives of multiculturalism.

Perhaps the work begun at Port Huron will be taken up once

again around the world, for the globalization of power, capital, and empire surely will globalize the stirrings of conscience and resistance. While the powers that be debate whether the world is dominated by a single superpower (the U.S. position) or is multipolar (the position of the French, the Chinese, and others), there is an alternative vision appearing among the millions of people who are involved in global justice, peace, human rights, and environmental movements—the vision of a future created through participatory democracy.

—Tom Hayden

June 2005

NOTES

1. Christopher Hitchens, "Where Aquarius Went," *New York Times Book Review*, Dec. 19, 2004.

2. Thomas Cahill, "The Price of Infallibility," *New York Times*, April 5, 2005.

3. See Tom Hayden and Dick Flacks, "The Port Huron Statement at 40," *The Nation*, Aug. 5 and Aug. 12, 2002; Tom Hayden, *Rebel: A Personal History of the Sixties* (Los Angeles: Red Hen, 2002); Todd Gitlin, *The Sixties: Years of Hope, Days of Rage* (New York: Bantam, 1987); Richard Flacks, *Making History: The American Left and the American Mind* (New York: Columbia University Press, 1988); James Miller, *Democracy Is in the Streets: From Port Huron to the Siege of Chicago* (New York: Simon and Schuster, 1987); and Kirkpatrick Sale, *SDS* (New York: Random House, 1973). See also the documentary film *Rebels with a Cause*, by Helen Garvy and Robert Pardon.

4. These distinctions are discussed elegantly in Flacks, *Making History*.

5. Paul Berman, *A Tale of Two Utopias: The Political Journey of the Generation of 1968* (New York: Norton, 1996), 54. Italics added to quote for emphasis.

6. At various times, Benjamin Franklin, Thomas Paine, and Thomas Jefferson wrote approvingly of Indian political customs. As one historian described Iroquois culture, there were "no laws or ordinances, sheriffs and constables, judges and juries, or courts or jails." These idyllic themes evolved into the later sixties communes, organic gardening and medicine, environmentalist lifestyles, and other practices. See Howard Zinn, *A People's History of the United States, 1492–Present* (1980; New York: Harper Collins, 2003), 1–23. John Adams wrote in 1787 that "to collect together the legislation of the Indians would take up much room but would be well worth pains," as cited in an excellent collection by Oren Lyons, John Mohawk, Vine Deloria, Laurence Hauptman, Howard Berman, Donald Grinde, Curtis Berkey, and Robert Venables, *Exiled in the Land of the Free: Democracy, Indian Nations, and the U.S. Constitution* (Santa Fe, N. Mex.: Clear Light, 1992), 109. The 1778 Articles of Confederation Congress actually proposed an Indian state headed by the Delaware nation (ibid., 113).

7. Thomas Paine, *Rights of Man* (1792; New York: Penguin, 1984), 70, 176.

8. In a Jefferson letter dated Feb. 2, 1816, cited by Berman, *Tale of Two Utopias,* 51.

9. John Dewey, quoted in Berman, *Tale of Two Utopias,* 53.

10. Retreating both from enlightenment beliefs in "infinite perfectibility" and negative beliefs in "original sin," the statement asserted that human beings are "infinitely precious" and possessed of "unfulfilled capacities for reason, freedom and love." The wording was provided by a Mexican-American Catholic activist, Maria Varela, who quoted from the copy of a Church encyclical she happened to carry. Casey Hayden spoke of those years as a "holy time."

11. Bob Dylan, *Chronicles,* vol. 1 (New York: Simon and Schuster, 2004), 34–35.

12. Sale, *SDS,* 27.

13. Ignazio Silone, *Bread and Wine* (1936; New York: Signet 1986); see also Miller, *Democracy Is in the Streets,* 53.

14. For example, the late Carl Wittman, who joined SDS shortly after Port Huron and worked with me as a community organizer in the Newark project, eventually came out of the closet to write "A Gay Manifesto," a defining document of the gay liberation movement, six years after Port Huron. See David Carter, *Stonewall: The Riots That Sparked the Gay Revolution* (New York: St. Martins, 2004), 118–19.

15. The phrase is that of Harvard professor Samuel Huntington in a speech to the elite Trilateral Commission in 1976 during the bicentennial of the Declaration of Independence. Huntington noted, "The 1960s witnessed a dramatic upsurge of democratic fervor in America," a trend he diagnosed as a "distemper" that threatened both governability and national security. Huntington proposed there be "limits to the extension of political democracy." See account in Zinn, *People's History*, 558–60.

16. The sudden reframing of America's relationship with the Soviet Union was described by Cyrus Sulzberger in the *New York Times* as follows: "The momentum of pro-Soviet feeling worked up during the war to support the Grand Alliance had continued too heavily after the armistice. This made it difficult for the administration to carry out the stiffer diplomatic policy required now. For this reason . . . a campaign was worked up to obtain a better balance of public opinion to permit the government to permit the government to adopt a harder line" (Mar. 21, 1946). Instead of seeking coexistence with the Soviet Union, the United States began talk of a "Cold War," an "iron curtain," and an "iron fist" instead of "babying the Soviets"; the Republican Party campaigned in 1946 on a platform of "Republicanism versus Communism," and the U.S. Chamber of Commerce collaborated with the FBI in distributing anticommunist materials, all *before* the Chinese communist revolution or Soviet testing of an atomic bomb. See Virginia Carmichael, *Framing History: The Rosenberg Story and the Cold War* (Minneapolis: University of Minnesota, 1993), 32–33.

17. See Paul Buhle, "How Sweet It Wasn't: The Scholars and the CIA," in

John McMillian and Paul Buhle, *The New Left Revisited* (Philadelphia: Temple University Press, 2003), 263.

18. See Todd Gitlin, *Letters to a Young Activist* (New York: Basic Books, 2003). Gitlin has not moved to the conservative camp but has been identified himself with "progressive patriotism," including use of military means to quell terrorism and denunciations of street demonstrators at places like the 2004 Republican convention. Oddly, his advice to the new radicals in *Letters* omits taking a position on the wars in Afghanistan and Iraq.

19. Buhle, "How Sweet It Wasn't," on the Committee on Cultural Freedom. In 1967, *Ramparts* magazine exposed the longtime CIA funding of the U.S. National Student Association. The CIA and State Department have long provided funding for international AFL-CIO projects designed to subvert radical labor movements in Latin America and elsewhere. According to U.S. Senate hearings held by Sen. Frank Church, the CIA funded several hundred academics on over two hundred campuses to "write books and other material to be used for propaganda purposes." See Zinn, *People's History*, 555–56.

20. Drafted in part by Michael Vester of the German SDS, then a student at Bowdoin College, the section on the Cold War foreshadowed the later movements to demilitarize Europe.

21. For my own account, see Hayden, *Rebel*, 79–84; or see Gitlin, *The Sixties*, 113–26.

22. See Lori Wallach and Patrick Woodall, *Whose Trade Organization? A Comprehensive Guide to the WTO* (New York: New Press, 2004).

23. The portion of America's gross national income given in foreign aid has declined by nearly 90 percent since the time of the *Port Huron Statement*, from 0.54 percent in 1962 to 0.16 percent in 2004, ranking the U.S. government behind twenty other nations. (Celia W. Dugger, "Discerning a New Course for World Donor Nations," *New York Times*, April 18, 2005).

24. Recent victims of the "soft on terrorism" charge were U.S. Senator Max

Cleland, a paraplegic Vietnam veteran, in 2002, and of course U.S. Senator and decorated Vietnam War hero John Kerry in the 2004 presidential race.

25. Taylor Branch, *Pillar of Fire: America in the King Years, 1963–64*, (New York: Simon and Schuster, 1998), 475–76.

26. At the time, Lewis was the chairman of the Student Nonviolent Coordinating Committee, the most radical and frontline civil rights organization. Attempts were made to edit and dilute his speech given at the March on Washington, which asked a good question: "Where is our party?" Later Lewis became an elected Atlanta congressman and prime sponsor of the Smithsonian's African-American Museum, near the spot where the 1963 march took place.

27. Jonathan Rosenberg and Zachary Karabell, *Kennedy, Johnson, and the Quest for Justice: The Civil Rights Tapes* (New York: Norton, 2003), 172.

28. ibid., 31.

29. The 63 percent disapproval of Freedom Rides is noted in Taylor Branch, *Parting the Waters: America in the King Years, 1954–63* (New York: Simon and Schuster, 1988), 478. *New York Times* editorial, Branch, 478 as well.

30. Rosenberg and Karabell, *Kennedy, Johnson, and the Quest*, 130.

31. Scott Stossel, *Sarge: The Life and Times of Sargeant Shriver* (Washington, D.C.: Smithsonian Books, 2004), 476.

32. Edwin O. Guthman and Jeffrey Shulman, *Robert Kennedy in His Own Words: The Unpublished Recollections of the Kennedy Years* (New York: Bantam, 1988), 300.

33. Richard Parker, *John Kenneth Galbraith: His Life, His Economics, His Politics* (New York: Farrar, Straus, Giroux, 2005), 405. James K. Galbraith, "Exit Strategy: In 1963, JFK ordered a complete withdrawal from Vietnam," *Boston Review*, October/November 1963. Robert McNamara confirmed Kennedy's plan for a complete withdrawal by 1965 in a speech at the LBJ Library on May 1, 1995, based on White House tapes. On

October 4, 1963, a memorandum from General Maxwell Taylor stated that "All planning will be directed towards preparing RVN [Republic of Vietnam] forces for the withdrawal of all U.S. special assistance units and personnel by the end of calendar year 1965." In a conversation with Daniel Ellsberg, Robert Kennedy stated, "We wanted to win if we could, but my brother was determined never to send ground troops to Vietnam . . . I do know what he intended. All I can say is that he was absolutely determined not to send ground units. . . . We would have fuzzed it up. We would have gotten a government that asked us out or that would have negotiated with the other side. We would have handled it like Laos." Daniel Ellsberg, *Secrets: A Memoir of Vietnam and the Pentagon Papers* (New York: Viking, 2002), 195. In an earlier, more ambiguous interview in 1964, while he was mulling his own thoughts about Vietnam, RFK gave noncommittal answers to John Barlow Martin: "Q: There was never any consideration given to pulling out? A: No. Q: But at the same time, no disposition to go in? A: No. Everybody, including General MacArthur, felt that land conflict between our troops—white troops and Asian— would only end in disaster." Guthman and Shulman, *Robert Kennedy*, 395. On these issues, I disagree with Noam Chomsky and numerous others who have claimed that LBJ's escalation of the war was simply a "continuation of Kennedy's policy," to quote Stanley Karnow as cited in Galbraith, "Exit Strategy."

34. Michael R. Beschloss, *Taking Charge: The Johnson White House Tapes, 1963–1964* (New York: Simon and Schuster, 1997), 439.

35. ibid., 508.

36. ibid., 455.

37. This is according to SNCC participants in the meeting.

38. Beschloss, *Taking Charge*, 534.

39. ibid., 532–33.

40. ibid., 546.

41. According to Daniel Ellsberg, then at the Pentagon, the president set up an inter-agency task force the day before the November 3 election to make plans for escalation. "It hadn't started a week earlier because its focus might have leaked to the voters . . . Moreover, we didn't start the work a day or week later, after the votes were cast, because there was no time to waste . . . It didn't matter that much to us what the public thought." Ellsberg, *Secrets*, 50–51.

42. See Kevin Phillips, *The Emerging Republican Majority* (New Rochelle, N.Y.: Arlington House, 1969).

43. Garry Wills, *Nixon Agonistes: The Crisis of the Self-Made Man* (New York: Signet, 1969), 327–33.

44. Garry Wills, *A Necessary Evil: A History of American Distrust of Government* (New York: Simon and Schuster, 1999), 289–98.

45. ibid., 293.

46. ibid.

47. Wills, *Nixon Agonistes*, 301.

48. Hayden, *Rebel*, 299.

49. In 2000, by comparison, I campaigned for Al Gore over the third-party campaign of Ralph Nader.

50. Sale, *SDS*.

51. Wills, 294.

52. Many of us were targeted for "neutralization" by the FBI. See Hayden, *Rebel*, for FBI documents. For declassified FBI counterintelligence documents against dissenters over the years, see Ward Churchill, Jim Vander Wall, *The Cointelpro Papers: Documents from the FBI's Secret Wars Against Dissent in the United States* (1990; Cambridge, Mass.: South End, 2002).

53. The "zigzag" accusation is from Berman, *Tale of Two Utopias*, 109.

54. One exemption to this rule is the National Organization for Women (NOW), which has managed to balance the catalytic and bureaucratic poles since its inception in 1965. Another is the Sierra Club. In both

cases, the grassroots membership plays a key role in the energy flow through the organizational machinery.

55. All figures in Zinn, *People's History*, 490–92.

56. The then-secret Pentagon Papers quote administration advisors in 1968 as saying "this growing disaffection, accompanied as it certainly will be, by increased defiance of the draft and growing unrest in the cities because of the belief that we are neglecting domestic problems, runs great risks of provoking a domestic crisis of unprecedented proportions." In his memoirs, President Nixon wrote: "although publicly I continued to ignore the raging antiwar controversy . . . I knew, however, that after all the protests and the Moratorium, American public opinion would be seriously divided by the war." Note that these concerns were based purely on cost/benefit calculations, not on moral or public policy grounds. In Zinn, *People's History*, 500, 501.

57. John Markoff, *What the Dormouse Said: How the Sixties Counterculture Shaped the Personal Computer Industry* (New York: Viking, 2005). See Andrew Leonard, "Book of the Times; California Dreaming: A True Story of Computers, Drugs and Rock 'n' Roll," *New York Times*, May 7, 2005.

58. From Senate hearings, in Zinn, *People's History*, 557. At the time, in 1961, I was writing a pamphlet on the civil rights movement for the U.S. National Student Association for international distribution. Without my knowledge, CIA funds were paying for it, presumably to show an idealistic image at international youth forums.

59. Kenneth Keniston, *Young Radicals: Notes on Committed Youth* (New York: Harcourt Brace, 1968), 235.

60. Lynne V. Cheney, *Telling the Truth* (New York: Touchstone, 1996), 33.

61. Richard Bradley, *Harvard Rules* (New York: HarperCollins, 2005). Quoted in *New York Times* review, March 27, 2005.

62. Kirby Dick and Amy Ziering Kofman, *Derrida: Screenplay and Essays on the Film* (New York: Routledge, 2005), 62.

63. Silone, *Bread and Wine*, 146.

INTRODUCTORY NOTE

THE FOLLOWING DOCUMENT, THE *PORT HURON STATEMENT*, was the first official statement of Students for a Democratic Society. Growing out of a draft statement prepared by SDS staff member Tom Hayden, the *Statement* represents the collective thought of the inspirational founding Convention of SDS, held in Port Huron, Michigan, June 11–15, 1962.

At the time of its writing, the Convention declared the *Port Huron Statement* to be "a living document open to change with our times and experiences." Since its adoption there have been changes in the American and world scenes, and changes in SDS as well. And although few of its original writers would agree today with all of its conclusions, it remains an essential source of SDS direction, a continual stimulus to thinking on campuses and in the movement, and one of the earliest embodiments of the feelings of the new movement of young people which began in the sixties.

First printing (mimeographed), 20,000—August 1962
Second printing, 20,000—December 1964

INTRODUCTION: AGENDA FOR A GENERATION

WE ARE PEOPLE OF THIS GENERATION, BRED IN AT LEAST modest comfort, housed now in universities, looking uncomfortably to the world we inherit.

When we were kids the United States was the wealthiest and strongest country in the world; the only one with the atom bomb, the least scarred by modern war, an initiator of the United Nations that we thought would distribute Western influence throughout the world. Freedom and equality for each individual, government of, by, and for the people—these American values we found good, principles by which we could live as men. Many of us began maturing in complacency.

As we grew, however, our comfort was penetrated by events too troubling to dismiss. First, the permeating and victimizing fact of human degradation, symbolized by the Southern struggle against racial bigotry, compelled most of us from silence to activism. Second, the enclosing fact of the Cold War, symbolized by the presence of the Bomb, brought awareness that we ourselves, and our friends, and millions of abstract "others" we knew more directly because of our common peril, might die at any time. We might deliberately ignore, or avoid, or fail to feel all other human problems, but not these two, for these were too immediate and crushing in their impact, too challenging in the demand that we as individuals take the responsibility for encounter and resolution.

While these and other problems either directly oppressed us or rankled our consciences and became our own subjective concerns, we began to see complicated and disturbing paradoxes in our surrounding America. The declaration "all men are created equal . . ." rang hollow before the facts of Negro life in the South and the big cities of the North. The proclaimed peaceful intentions of the United States contradicted its economic and military investments in the Cold War status quo.

We witnessed, and continue to witness, other paradoxes. With nuclear energy whole cities can easily be powered, yet the dominant nation-states seem more likely to unleash destruction greater than that incurred in all wars of human history. Although our own technology is destroying old and creating new forms of social organization, men still tolerate meaningless work and idleness. While two-thirds of mankind suffers undernourishment, our own upper classes revel amidst superfluous abundance. Although world population is expected to double in forty years, the nations still tolerate anarchy as a major principle of international conduct and uncontrolled exploitation governs the sapping of the earth's physical resources. Although mankind desperately needs revolutionary leadership, America rests in national stalemate, its goals ambiguous and tradition-bound instead of informed and clear, its democratic system apathetic and manipulated rather than "of, by, and for the people."

Not only did tarnish appear on our image of American virtue, not only did disillusion occur when the hypocrisy of American ideals was discovered, but we began to sense that what we had originally seen as the American Golden Age was actually the decline of an era. The worldwide outbreak of revolution against colonialism and imperialism, the entrenchment of totalitarian states, the menace of war, overpopulation, international disorder, supertechnology—these trends were testing the tenacity of our own commitment to democracy and freedom and our abilities to visualize their application to a world in upheaval.

Our work is guided by the sense that we may be the last generation in the experiment with living. But we are a minority— the vast majority of our people regard the temporary equilibriums of our society and world as eternally-functional parts. In this is perhaps the outstanding paradox: we ourselves are imbued with urgency, yet the message of our society is that there is no viable alternative to the present. Beneath the reassuring tones of the politicians, beneath the common opinion that America will "muddle through," beneath the stagnation of those who have closed their minds to the future, is the pervading feeling that there simply are no alternatives, that our times have witnessed the exhaustion not only of Utopias, but of any new departures as well. Feeling the press of complexity upon the emptiness of life, people are fearful of the thought that at any moment things might be thrust out of control. They fear change itself, since change might smash whatever invisible framework seems to hold back chaos for them now. For most Americans, all crusades are suspect, threatening. The fact that each individual sees apathy in his fellows perpetuates the common reluctance to organize for change. The dominant institutions are complex enough to blunt the minds of their potential critics, and entrenched enough to swiftly dissipate or entirely repel the energies of protest and reform, thus limiting human expectancies. Then, too, we are a materially improved society, and by our own improvements we seem to have weakened the case for further change.

Some would have us believe that Americans feel contentment amidst prosperity—but might it not be better called a glaze above deeply-felt anxieties about their role in the new world? And if these anxieties produce a developed indifference to human affairs, do they not as well produce a yearning to believe there *is* an alternative to the present, that something *can* be done to change circumstances in the school, the workplaces, the bureaucracies, the government? It is to this latter yearning, at once the spark and engine of change, that we direct our present appeal. The search for truly democratic alternatives to the present, and a commitment to social experimentation with them, is a worthy and fulfilling human enterprise, one which moves us and, we hope, others today. On such a basis do we offer this document of our convictions and analysis: as an effort in understanding and changing the conditions of humanity in the late twentieth century, an effort rooted in the ancient, still unfulfilled conception of man attaining determining influence over his circumstances of life.

VALUES

MAKING VALUES EXPLICIT—AN INITIAL TASK IN ESTABLISHING alternatives—is an activity that has been devalued and corrupted. The conventional moral terms of the age, the politician moralities—"free world," "people's democracies"—reflect realities poorly, if at all, and seem to function more as ruling myths than as descriptive principles. But neither has our experience in the universities brought us moral enlightenment. Our professors and administrators sacrifice controversy to public relations; their curriculums change more slowly than the living events of the world; their skills and silence are purchased by investors in the arms race; passion is called unscholastic. The questions we might want raised—what is really important? can we live in a different and better way? if we wanted to change society, how would we do it?—are not thought to be questions of a "fruitful, empirical nature," and thus are brushed aside.

Unlike youth in other countries we are used to moral

leadership being exercised and moral dimensions being clarified by our elders. But today, for us, not even the liberal and socialist preachments of the past seem adequate to the forms of the present. Consider the old slogans: Capitalism Cannot Reform Itself, United Front Against Fascism, General Strike, All Out on May Day. Or, more recently, No Cooperation with Commies and Fellow Travellers, Ideologies are Exhausted, Bipartisanship, No Utopias. These are incomplete, and there are few new prophets. It has been said that our liberal and socialist predecessors were plagued by vision without program, while our own generation is plagued by program without vision. All around us there is astute grasp of method, technique—the committee, the ad hoc group, the lobbyist, the hard and soft sell, the make, the projected image—but, if pressed critically, such expertise is incompetent to explain its implicit ideals. It is highly fashionable to identify oneself by old categories, or by naming a respected political figure, or by explaining "how we would vote" on various issues.

Theoretic chaos has replaced the idealistic thinking of old—and, unable to reconstitute theoretic order, men have condemned idealism itself. Doubt has replaced hopefulness—and men act out a defeatism that is labelled realistic. The decline of utopia and hope is in fact one of the defining features of social life today. The reasons are various: the dreams of the older left were perverted by Stalinism and never recreated; the congressional stalemate makes men narrow their view of the possible; the specialization of human activity leaves little room for sweeping thought; the horrors of the twentieth century, symbolized in the gas-ovens and concentration camps and atom bombs, have blasted hopefulness. To be idealistic is to be considered apocalyptic, deluded. To have no serious aspirations, on the contrary, is to be "toughminded."

In suggesting social goals and values, therefore, we are aware of entering a sphere of some disrepute. Perhaps matured by the past, we have no sure formulas, no closed theories — but that does not mean values are beyond discussion and tentative determination. A first task of any social movement is to convince people that the search for orienting theories and the creation of human values is complex but worthwhile. We are aware that to avoid platitudes we must analyze the concrete conditions of social order. But to direct such an analysis we must use the guideposts of basic principles. Our own social values involve conceptions of human beings, human relationships, and social systems.

We regard *men* as infinitely precious and possessed of unfulfilled capacities for reason, freedom, and love. In affirming these principles we are aware of countering perhaps the dominant conceptions of man in the twentieth century: that he is a thing to be manipulated, and that he is inherently incapable of directing his own affairs. We oppose the depersonalization that reduces human beings to the status of things — if anything, the brutalities of the twentieth century teach that means and ends are intimately related, that vague appeals to "posterity" cannot justify the mutilations of the present. We oppose, too, the doctrine of human incompetence because it rests essentially on the modern fact that men have been "competently" manipulated into incompetence — we see little reason why men cannot meet with increasing skill the complexities and responsibilities of their situation, if society is organized not for minority, but for majority, participation in decision-making.

Men have unrealized potential for self-cultivation, self-direction, self-understanding, and creativity. It is this potential that we regard as crucial and to which we appeal, not to the human potentiality for violence, unreason, and submission to authority. The goal of man and society should be human independence: a concern not with image of popularity but with finding a meaning in life that is personally authentic; a quality of mind not compulsively driven by a sense of powerlessness, nor one which unthinkingly adopts status values, nor one which represses all threats to its habits, but one which has full, spontaneous access to present and past experiences, one which easily unites the fragmented parts of personal history, one which openly faces problems which are troubling and unresolved; one with an intuitive awareness of possibilities, an active sense of curiosity, an ability and willingness to learn.

This kind of independence does not mean egotistic individualism—the object is not to have one's way so much as it is to have a way that is one's own. Nor do we deify man—we merely have faith in his potential.

Human relationships should involve fraternity and honesty. Human interdependence is contemporary fact; human brotherhood must be willed, however, as a condition of future survival and as the most appropriate form of social relations. Personal links between man and man are needed, especially to go beyond the partial and fragmentary bonds of function that bind men only as worker to worker, employer to employee, teacher to student, American to Russian.

Loneliness, estrangement, isolation describe the vast distance between man and man today. These dominant tendencies cannot be overcome by better personnel management, nor by improved gadgets, but only when a love of man overcomes the idolotrous worship of things by man. As the individualism we affirm is not egoism, the selflessness we affirm is not self-elimination. On the contrary we, believe in generosity of a kind that imprints one's unique individual qualities in the relation to other men, and to all human activity. Further, to dislike isolation is not to favor the abolition of privacy; the latter differs from isolation in that it occurs or is abolished according to individual will.

We would replace power rooted in possession, privilege, or circumstances by power and uniqueness rooted in love, relectiveness, reason, and creativity. As a *social system* we seek the establishment of a democracy of individual participation, governed by two central aims: that the individual share in those social decisions determining the quality and direction of his life; that society be organized to encourage independence in men and provide the media for their common participation.

In a participatory democracy, the political life would be based in several root principles:

that decision-making of basic social consequence be carried on by public groupings;

that politics be seen positively, as the art of collectively creating an acceptable pattern of social relations;

that politics has the function of bringing people out of isolation and into community, thus being a necessary, though not sufficient, means of finding meaning in personal life;

that the political order should serve to clarify problems in a way instrumental to their solution; it should provide outlets for the expression of personal grievance and aspiration; opposing views should be organized so as to illuminate choices and facilitate the attainment of goals; channels should be commonly available, to relate men to knowledge and to power so that private problems—from bad recreation facilities to personal alienation—are formulated as general issues.

The economic sphere would have as its basis the principles:

that work should involve incentives worthier than money or survival. It should be educative, not stultifying; creative, not mechanical; self-directed, not manipulated, encouraging independence, a respect for others, a sense of dignity and a willingness to accept social responsibility, since it is this experience that has crucial influence on habits, perceptions and individual ethics;

that the economic experience is so personally decisive that the individual must share in its full determination;

that the economy itself is of such social importance that its major resources and means of production should be open to democratic participation and subject to democratic regulation.

Like the political and economic ones, major social institutions—cultural, educational, rehabilitative, and others—should be generally organized with the well-being and dignity of man as the essential measure of success.

In social change or interchange, we find violence to be abhorrent because it requires generally the transformation of the target, be it a human being or a community of people, into a depersonalized object of hate. It is imperative that the means of violence be abolished and the institutions—local, national, international—that encourage nonviolence as a condition of conflict be developed.

These are our central values, in skeletal form. It remains vital to understand their denial or attainment in the context of the modern world.

THE STUDENTS

In the last few years, thousands of American students demonstrated that they at least felt the urgency of the times. They moved actively and directly against racial injustices, the threat of war, violations of individual rights of conscience and, less frequently, against economic manipulation. They succeeded in restoring a small measure of controversy to the campuses after the stillness of the McCarthy period. They succeeded, too, in gaining some concessions from the people and institutions they opposed, especially in the fight against racial bigotry.

The significance of these scattered movements lies not in their success or failure in gaining objectives—at least not yet. Nor does the significance lie in the intellectual "competence" or "maturity" of the students involved—as some pedantic elders allege. The significance is in the fact the students are breaking the crust of apathy and overcoming the inner alienation that remain the defining characteristics of American college life.

If student movements for change are still rareties on the campus scene, what is commonplace there? The real campus, the familiar campus, is a place of private people, engaged in their notorious "inner emigration." It is a place of commitment to business-as-usual, getting ahead, playing it cool. It is a place of mass affirmation of the Twist, but mass reluctance toward the controversial public stance. Rules are accepted as "inevitable," bureaucracy as "just circumstances," irrelevance as "scholarship," selflessness as "martyrdom," politics as "just another way to make people, and an unprofitable one, too."

Almost no students value activity as citizens. Passive in public, they are hardly more idealistic in arranging their private lives: Gallup concludes they will settle for "low success, and won't risk high failure." There is not much willingness to take risks (not even in business), no setting of dangerous goals, no real conception of personal identity except one manufactured in the image of others, no real urge for personal fulfillment except to be almost as successful as the very successful people. Attention is being paid to social status (the quality of shirt collars, meeting people, getting wives or husbands, making solid contacts for later on); much, too, is paid to academic status (grades, honors, the med school rat race). But neglected generally is real intellectual status, the personal cultivation of the mind.

"Students don't even give a damn about the apathy," one has said. Apathy toward apathy begets a privately-constructed universe, a place of systematic study schedules, two nights each week for beer, a girl or two, and early marriage; a framework infused with personality, warmth, and under control, no matter how unsatisfying otherwise.

Under these conditions university life loses all relevance to some. Four hundred thousand of our classmates leave college every year.

But apathy is not simply an attitude; it is a product of social institutions, and of the structure and organization of higher education itself.

The extracurricular life is ordered according to *in loco parentis* theory, which ratifies the administration as the moral guardian of the young.

The accompanying "let's pretend" theory of student extracurricular affairs validates student government as a training center for those who want to spend their lives in political pretense, and discourages initiative from the more articulate, honest, and sensitive students. The bounds and style of controversy are delimited before controversy begins. The university "prepares" the student for "citizenship" through perpetual rehearsals and, usually, through emasculation of what creative spirit there is in the individual.

The academic life contains reinforcing counterparts to the way in which extracurricular life is organized. The academic world is founded on a teacher-student relation analogous to the parent-child relation which characterizes *in loco parentis*. Further, academia includes a radical separation of the student from the material of study. That which is studied, the social reality, is "objectified" to sterility, dividing the student from life—just as he is restrained in active involvement controlling student government. The specialization of function and knowledge, admittedly necessary to our complex technological and social structure, has produced an exaggerated compartmentalization of study and understanding. This has contributed to an overly parochial view, by faculty, of the role of its research and scholarship, to a discontinuous and truncated understanding, by students, of the surrounding social order; and to a loss of personal attachment, by nearly all, to the worth of study as a humanistic enterprise.

There is, finally, the cumbersome academic bureaucracy extending throughout the academic as well as the extracurricular structures, contributing to the sense of outer complexity and inner powerlessness that transforms the honest searching of many students to a ratification of convention and, worse, to a numbness to present and future catastrophes. The size and financing systems of the university enhance the permanent trusteeship of the administrative bureaucracy, their power leading to a shift within the university toward the value standards of business and the administrative mentality. Huge foundations and other private financial interests shape the under-financed colleges and universities, not only making them more commercial, but less disposed to diagnose society critically, less open to dissent. Many social and physical scientists, neglecting the liberating heritage of higher learning, develop "human relations" or "morale-producing" techniques for the corporate economy, while others exercise their intellectual skills to accelerate the arms race.

Tragically, the university could serve as a significant source of social criticism and an initiator of new modes and molders of attitudes. But the actual intellectual effect of the college experience is hardly distinguishable from that of any other communications channel—say, a television set—passing on the stock truths of the day. Students leave college somewhat more "tolerant" than when they arrived, but basically unchallenged in

their values and political orientations. With administrators or-
dering the institution, and faculty the curriculum, the student
learns by his isolation to accept elite rule within the university,
which prepares him to accept later forms of minority control.
The real function of the educational system—as opposed to its
more rhetorical function of "searching for truth"—is to impart
the key information and styles that will help the student get by,
modestly but comfortably, in the big society beyond.

THE SOCIETY BEYOND

Look beyond the campus, to America itself. That student life is more intellectual, and perhaps more comfortable, does not obscure the fact that the fundamental qualities of life on the campus reflect the habits of society at large. The fraternity president is seen at the junior manager levels; the sorority queen has gone to Grosse Pointe; the serious poet burns for a place, any place, to work; the once-serious and never-serious poets work at the advertising agencies. The desperation of people threatened by forces about which they know little and of which they can say less; the cheerful emptiness of people "giving up" all hope of changing things; the faceless ones polled by Gallup who listed "international affairs" fourteenth on their list of "problems" but who also expected thermonuclear war in the next few years; in these and other forms, Americans are in withdrawal from public life, from any collective effort at directing their own affairs.

Some regard these national doldrums as a sign of healthy

approval of the established order—but is it approval by consent or manipulated acquiescence? Others declare that the people are withdrawn because compelling issues are fast disappearing—perhaps there are fewer breadlines in America, but is Jim Crow gone, is there enough work and work more fulfilling, is world war a diminishing threat, and what of the revolutionary new peoples? Still others think the national quietude is a necessary consequence of the need for elites to resolve complex and specialized problems of modern industrial society—but, then, why should *business* elites help decide foreign policy, and who controls the elites anyway, and are they solving mankind's problems? Others, finally, shrug knowingly and announce that full democracy never worked anywhere in the past—but why lump qualitatively different civilizations together, and how can a social order work well if its best thinkers are skeptics, and is man really doomed forever to the domination of today?

There are no convincing apologies for the contemporary malaise. While the world tumbles toward the final war, while men in other nations are trying desperately to alter events, while the very future qua future is uncertain—America is without community, impulse, without the inner momentum necessary for an age when societies cannot successfully perpetuate themselves by their military weapons, when democracy must be viable because of the quality of life, not its quantity of rockets.

The apathy here is, first *subjective*—the felt powerlessness of ordinary people, the resignation before the enormity of events. But subjective apathy is encouraged by the *objective* American situation—the actual structural separation of people from power, from relevant knowledge, from pinnacles of decision-making. Just as the university influences the student way of life, so do major social institutions create the circumstances in which the isolated citizen will try hopelessly to understand his world and himself.

The very isolation of the individual—from power and community and ability to aspire—means the rise of a democracy without publics. With the great mass of people structurally remote and psychologically hesitant with respect to democratic institutions, those institutions themselves attenuate and become, in the fashion of the vicious circle, progressively less accessible to those few who aspire to serious participation in social affairs. The vital democratic connection between community and leadership, between the mass and the several elites, has been so wrenched, and perverted that disastrous policies go unchallenged time and again.

POLITICS WITHOUT PUBLICS

THE AMERICAN POLITICAL SYSTEM IS NOT THE DEMOCRATIC model of which its glorifiers speak. In actuality it frustrates democracy by confusing the individual citizen, paralyzing policy discussion, and consolidating the irresponsible power of military and business interests.

A crucial feature of the political apparatus in America is that greater differences are harbored within each major party than the differences existing between them. Instead of two parties presenting distinctive and significant differences of approach, what dominates the system is a natural interlocking of Democrats from Southern states with the more conservative elements of the Republican party. This arrangement of forces is blessed by the seniority system of Congress which guarantees congressional committee domination by conservatives—10 of 17 committees in the Senate and 13 of 21 in the House of Representatives are chaired currently by Dixiecrats.

The party overlap, however, is not the only structural antagonist of democracy in politics. First, the localized nature of the party system does not encourage discussion of national and international issues: thus problems are not raised by and for people, and political representatives usually are unfettered from any responsibilities to the general public except those regarding parochial matters. Second, whole constituencies are divested of the full political power they might have: many Negroes in the South are prevented from voting, migrant workers are disenfranchised by various residence requirements, some urban and suburban dwellers are victimized by gerrymandering, and poor people are too often without the power to obtain political representation. Third, the focus of political attention is significantly distorted by the enormous lobby force, composed predominantly of business interests, spending hundreds of millions each year in an attempt to conform facts about productivity, agriculture, defense, and social services, to the wants of private economic groupings.

What emerges from the party contradiction and insulation of privately-held power is the organized political stalemate: calcification dominates flexibility as the principle of parliamentary organization, frustration is the expectancy of legislators intending liberal reform, and Congress becomes less and less central to national decision-making, especially in the area of foreign policy. In this context, confusion and blurring is built into the formulation of issues, long-range priorities are not discussed in the rational manner needed for policy-making, the politics of personality and "image" become a more important mechanism than the construction of issues in a way that affords each voter a challenging and real option. The American voter is buffeted from all directions by pseudo-problems, by the structurally-initiated sense that nothing political is subject to human mastery. Worried by his mundane problems which never get solved, but constrained by the common belief that politics is an agonizingly slow accommodation of views, he quits all pretense of bothering.

A most alarming fact is that few, if any, politicians are calling for changes in these conditions. Only a handful even are calling on the President to "live up to" platform pledges; no one is demanding structural changes, such as the shuttling of Southern Democrats out of the Democratic Party. Rather than protesting the state of politics, most politicians are reinforcing and aggravating that state. While in practice they rig public opinion to suit their own interests, in word and ritual they enshrine "the sovereign public" and call for more and more letters. Their speeches and campaign actions are banal, based on a degrading conception of what people want to hear. They respond not to dialogue, but to pressure: and knowing this, the ordinary citizen sees even greater inclination to shun the political sphere. The politician is usually a trumpeter to "citizenship" and "service to the nation," but since he is unwilling to seriously rearrange power relationships, his trumpetings only increase apathy by creating no outlets. Much of the time the call to "service" is justified not in idealistic terms, but in the crasser terms of "defending the free world from communism" — thus making future idealistic impulses harder to justify in anything but Cold War terms.

In such a setting of status quo politics, where most if not all government activity is rationalized in Cold War anti-communist terms, it is somewhat natural that discontented,

super-patriotic groups would emerge through political channels and explain their ultra-conservatism as the best means
of Victory Over Communism. They have become a politically influential force within the Republican Party, at a
national level through Senator Goldwater, and at a local
level through their important social and economic roles.
Their political views are defined generally as the opposite of
the supposed views of communists: complete individual
freedom in the economic sphere, non-participation by the
government in the machinery of production. But actually
"anti-communism" becomes an umbrella by which to
protest liberalism, internationalism, welfareism, the active
civil rights and labor movements. It is to the disgrace of the
United States that such a movement should become a
prominent kind of public participation in the modern
world—but, ironically, it is somewhat to the interests of the
United States that such a movement should be a public con-
stituency pointed toward realignment of the political parties,
demanding a conservative Republican Party in the South
and an exclusion of the "leftist" elements of the national GOP.

THE ECONOMY

AMERICAN CAPITALISM TODAY ADVERTISES ITSELF AS THE Welfare State. Many of us comfortably expect pensions, medical care, unemployment compensation, and other social services in our lifetimes. Even with one-fourth of our productive capacity unused, the majority of Americans are living in relative comfort—although their nagging incentive to "keep up" makes them continually dissatisfied with their possessions. In many places, unrestrained bosses, uncontrolled machines, and sweatshop conditions have been reformed or abolished and suffering tremendously relieved. But in spite of the benign yet obscuring effects of the New Deal reforms and the reassuring phrases of government economists and politicians, the paradoxes and myths of the economy are sufficient to irritate our complacency and reveal to us some essential causes of the American malaise.

We live amidst a national celebration of economic prosperity while poverty and deprivation remain an unbreakable way of life for millions in the "affluent society," including many of our own generation. We hear glib references to the "welfare state," "free enterprise," and "shareholder's democracy" while military defense is the main item of "public" spending and obvious oligopoly and other forms of minority rule defy real individual initiative or popular control. Work, too, is often unfulfilling and victimizing, accepted as a channel to status or plenty, if not a way to pay the bills, rarely as a means of understanding and controlling self and events. In work and leisure the individual is regulated as part of the system, a consuming unit, bombarded by hard-sell, soft-sell, lies and semi-true appeals to his basest drives. He is always told that he is a "free" man because of "free enterprise."

THE REMOTE CONTROL ECONOMY. We are subject to a remote control economy, which excludes the mass of individual "units"—the people—from basic decisions affecting the nature and organization of work, rewards, and opportunities. The modern concentration of wealth is fantastic. The wealthiest 1 percent of Americans own more than 80 percent of all personal shares of stock.[1] From World War II until the mid-fifties, the 50 biggest corporations increased their manufacturing production from 17 to 23 percent of the national total, and the share of the largest 200 companies rose from 30 to 37 percent.

---

[1] Statistics on wealth reveal the "have" and "have not" gap at home. Only 5 percent of all those in the $5,000 or less bracket own any stock at all. In 1953, personally-owned wealth in the U.S. stood at $1 trillion. Of this sum, $309.2 billion (30.2 percent) was owned by 1,659,000 top wealth-holders (with incomes of $60,000 or more). This elite comprised 1.04 percent of the population. Their average gross estate estimate was $182,000, as against the

To regard the various decisions of these elites as purely economic is shortsighted: their decisions affect in a momentous way the entire fabric of social life in America. Foreign investments influence political policies in underdeveloped areas—and our efforts to build a "profitable" capitalist world blind our foreign policy to mankind's needs and destiny. The drive for sales spurs phenomenal advertising efforts; the ethical drug industry, for instance, spent more than $750 million on promotions in 1960, nearly four times the amount available to all American medical schools for their educational programs. The arts, too, are organized substantially according to their commercial appeal; aesthetic values are subordinated to exchange values, and writers swiftly learn to consider the commercial market as much as the humanistic marketplace of ideas. The tendency to overproduction, to gluts of surplus commodities, encourages "market research" techniques to deliberately create pseudo-needs in consumers—we learn to buy "smart" things, regardless of their utility—and introduces wasteful "planned obsolescence" as a permanent feature of business strategy. While real social needs accumulate as rapidly as profits, it becomes evident that Money, instead of dignity of character, remains a pivotal American value and Profitability, instead of social use, a pivotal standard in determining priorities of resource allocation.

---

national average of $10,000. They held 80 percent of all corporation stock, virtually all state and local bonds and between 10 and 33 percent of other types of property: bonds, real estate, mortgages, life insurance, unincorporated businesses, and cash. They receive 40 percent of property, income-rent, interest dividends. The size of this elite's wealth has been relatively constant: 31.6% (1922). 30.6% (1939), 29.8% (1949), 30.2% (1958).

Within existing arrangements, the American business community cannot be said to encourage a democratic process nationally. Economic minorities not responsible to a public in any democratic fashion make decisions of a more profound importance than even those made by Congress. Such a claim is usually dismissed by respectful and knowing citations of the ways in which government asserts itself as keeper of the public interest at times of business irresponsibility. But the real, as opposed to the mythical, range of government "control" of the economy includes only:

1. some limited "regulatory" powers—which usually just ratify industry policies or serve as palliatives at the margins of significant business activity;

2. fiscal policy built upon defense expenditures as pump-priming "public works"—without a significant emphasis on peaceful "public works" to meet social priorities and alleviate personal hardships;

3. limited fiscal and monetary weapons which are rigid and have only minor effects, and are greatly limited by corporate veto: tax cuts and reforms; interest rate control (used generally to tug on investment but hurting the little investor most); tariffs which protect noncompetitive industries with political power and which keep less-favored nations out of the large trade mainstream, as the removal of barriers reciprocally with the Common Market may do disastrously to emerging countries outside of Europe: wage arbitration, the use of government coercion

in the name of "public interest" to hide the tensions between workers and business production controllers; price controls, which further maintain the status quo of big ownership and flushes out little investors for the sake of "stability";

4. very limited "poverty-solving" which is designed for the organized working class but not the shut-out, poverty-stricken migrants, farm workers, the indigent unaware of medical care or the lower-middle class person riddled with medical bills, the "unhireables" of minority groups or workers over 45 years of age, etc.;

5. regional development programs—such as the Area Redevelopment Act—which have been only "trickle down" welfare programs without broad authority for regional planning and development and public works spending. The federal highway program has been more significant than the "depressed areas" program in meeting the needs of people, but it is generally too remote and does not reach the vicious circle of poverty itself.

In short, the theory of government's "countervailing" business neglects the extent to which government influence is marginal to the basic production decisions, the basic decision-making environment of society, the basic structure of distribution and allocation which is still determined by major corporations with power and wealth concentrated among the few. A conscious conspiracy—as in the case of price-rigging in the electrical industry—is by no means generally or continuously operative but power undeniably does rest in comparative insulation from the public and its political representatives.

THE MILITARY-INDUSTRIAL COMPLEX. The most spectacular and important creation of the authoritarian and oligopolistic structure of economic decision-making in America is the institution called "the military-industrial complex" by former President Eisenhower—the powerful congruence of interest and structure among military and business elites which affects so much of our development and destiny. Not only is ours the first generation to live with the possibility of worldwide cataclysm—it is the first to experience the actual social preparation for cataclysm, the general militarization of American society. In 1948 Congress established Universal Military Training, the first peacetime conscription. The military became a permanent institution. Four years earlier, General Motors' Charles E. Wilson had heralded the creation of what he called the "permanent war economy," the continuous use of military spending as a solution to economic problems unsolved before the post-war boom, most notably the problem of the seventeen million jobless after eight years of the New Deal. This has left a "hidden crisis" in the allocation of resources by the American economy.

Since our childhood these two trends—the rise of the military and the installation of a defense-based economy—have grown fantastically. The Department of Defense, ironically the world's largest single organization, is worth $160 billion, owns 32 million acres of America and employs half the 7.5 million persons directly dependent on the military for subsistence, has an $11 billion payroll which is larger than the net annual income of all American corporations. Defense spending in the Eisenhower era totaled $350 billion and President Kennedy entered office pledging to go even beyond the present defense allocation of 60 cents from every public dollar spent. Except for a war-induced boom immediately after "our side" bombed Hiroshima, American economic prosperity has coincided with a growing dependence on military outlay—from 1941 to 1959 America's Gross National Product of $5.25 trillion included $700 billion in goods and services purchased for the defense effort, about one-seventh of the accumulated GNP. This pattern has included the steady concentration of military spending among a few corporations. In 1961, 86 percent of Defense Department contracts were awarded without competition. The ordnance industry of 100,000 people is completely engaged in military work; in the aircraft industry, 94 percent of 750,000 workers are linked to the war economy; shipbuilding, radio and communications equipment industries commit 40 percent of their work to defense; iron and steel, petroleum, metal-stamping and machine shop products, motors and generators, tools and hardware, copper, aluminum, and machine tools industries all devote at least 10 percent of their work to the same cause.

The intermingling of Big Military and Big Industry is evidenced in the 1,400 former officers working for the 100 corporations who received nearly all the $21 billion spent in procurement by the Defense Department in 1961. The overlap is most poignantly clear in the case of General Dynamics, the company which received the best 1961 contracts, employed the most retired officers (187), and is directed by a former Secretary of the Army. A *Fortune* magazine profile of General

Dynamics said: "The unique group of men who run Dynamics are only incidentally in rivalry with other U.S. manufacturers, with many of whom they actually act in concert. Their chief competitor is the USSR. The core of General Dynamics' corporate philosophy is the conviction that national defense is a more or less permanent business." Little has changed since Wilson's proud declaration of the Permanent War Economy back in the 1944 days when the top 200 corporations possessed 80 percent of all active prime war-supply contracts.

MILITARY-INDUSTRIAL POLITICS. The military and its supporting business foundation have found numerous forms of political expression, and we have heard their din endlessly. There has not been a major Congressional split on the issue of continued defense spending spirals in our lifetime. The triangular relations of the business, military, and political arenas cannot be better expressed than in Dixiecrat Carl Vinson's remarks as his House Armed Services Committee reported out a military construction bill of $808 million throughout the 50 states, for 1960-61: "There is something in this bill for everyone," he announced. President Kennedy had earlier acknowledged the valuable anti-recession features of the bill.

Imagine, on the other hand, $808 million suggested as an antirecession measure, but being poured into programs of social welfare: the impossibility of receiving support for such a measure identifies a crucial feature of defense spending—it is beneficial to private enterprise, while welfare spending is not. Defense spending does not "compete" with the private sector; it contains a natural obsolescence; its "confidential" nature permits easier boondoggling; the tax burdens to which it leads can be shunted from corporation to consumer as a "cost of production." Welfare spending, however, involves the government in competition with private corporations and contractors; it conflicts with immediate interests of private pressure groups; it leads to taxes on business. Think of the opposition of private power companies to current proposals for river and valley development, or the hostility of the real estate lobby to urban renewal; or the attitude of the American Medical Association to a paltry medical care bill; or of all business lobbyists to foreign aid; these are the pressures leading to the schizophrenic public-military, private-civilian economy of our epoch. The politicians, of course, take the line of least resistance and thickest support: warfare, instead of welfare, is easiest to stand up for: after all, the Free World is at stake (and our constituency's investments, too).

AUTOMATION, ABUNDANCE, AND CHALLENGE. But while the economy remains relatively static in its setting of priorities and allocation of resources, new conditions are emerging with enormous implications: the revolution of automation, and the replacement of scarcity by the potential of material abundance.

Automation, the process of machines replacing men in performing sensory, motoric, and complex logical tasks, is transforming society in ways that are scarcely comprehensible. By 1959, industrial production regained its 1957 "pre-recession" level—but with 750,000 fewer workers required. In the fifties as a whole, national production enlarged by 43 percent but the number of factory employees remained stationary, seven-tenths of one percent higher than in 1947.[2] Automation is destroying whole categories of work—impersonal thinkers have efficiently labeled this "structural unemployment"—in blue-collar, service, and even middle management occupations. In addition it is eliminating employment opportunities for a youth force that numbers one million more than it did in 1950, and rendering work far more difficult both to find and do for people in their forties and up. The consequences of this economic drama, strengthened by the force of post-war recessions, are momentous: five million becomes an acceptable unemployment tabulation, and misery, uprootedness, and anxiety become the lot of increasing numbers of Americans.

But while automation is creating social dislocation of a stunning kind, it paradoxically is imparting the opportunity for men the world around to rise in dignity from their knees. The dominant optimistic economic fact of this epoch is that fewer hands are needed now in actual production, although more goods and services are a real potentiality. The world could be fed, poverty abolished, the great public needs could be met, the brutish world of Darwinian scarcity could be brushed away, all men could have more time to pursue their leisure, drudgery in work could be cut to a minimum, education could become more of a

---

[2]The electronics industry lost 200,000 of 900,000 workers in the years 1953–57. In the steel industry, productive capacity has increased 20 percent since 1955, while the number of workers has fallen 17,000. Employment in the auto industry has decreased in the same period from 746,000 to 614,000. The chemical industry has enlarged its productive powers 27 percent although its work force has dropped by 3 percent. A farmer in 1962 can grow enough to feed 24 people, where one generation ago only 12 could be nourished. The United States Bureau of the Census used 50 statisticians in 1960 to perform the service that required 4,100 in 1950.

continuing process for all people, both public and personal needs could be met rationally But only in a system with selfish production motives and elitist control, a system which is less welfare than war-based, undemocratic rather than "stock-holder participative" as "sold to us," does the potentiality for abundance become a curse and a cruel irony:

1. Automation brings unemployment instead of more leisure for all and greater achievement of needs for all people in the world—a crisis instead of economic utopia. Instead of being introduced into a social system in a planned and equitable way, automation is initiated according to its profitability. The American Telephone and Telegraph holds back modern telephone equipment, invented with public research funds, until present equipment is *financially* unprofitable. Colleges develop teaching machines, mass-class techniques, and TV education to replace teachers: not to proliferate knowledge or to assist the qualified professors now, but to *"cut inefficiency* and become less *wasteful."* Technology, which could be a blessing to society, becomes more and more a sinister threat to humanistic and rational enterprise.

2. Hardcore poverty exists just beyond the neon lights of affluence, and the "have-nots" may be driven still further from opportunity as the high-technology society demands better education to get into the production mainstream and more capital investment to get into "business." Poverty is shameful in that it herds people by race, region, and previous condition of misfortune into

"uneconomic classes" in the so-called free society—the marginal worker is made more insecure by automation, high education requirements, heavier competition for jobs, the maintenance of low wages, and a high level of unemployment. People in the rut of poverty are strikingly unable to overcome the collection of forces working against them: poor health, bad neighborhoods, miserable schools, inadequate "welfare" services, unemployment and underemployment, weak political and union organization.

3. Surplus and potential plenty are wasted domestically and producers suffer impoverishment because the real needs of the world and of our society are not reflected in the market. Our huge bins of decomposing grain are classic American examples, as is the steel industry which, in the summer of 1962, is producing at 53 percent of capacity.

THE STANCE OF LABOR. Amidst all this, what of organized labor, the historic institutional representative of the exploited, the presumed "countervailing power" against the excesses of Big Business? The contemporary social assault on the labor movement is of crisis proportions. To the average American, "big labor" is a growing cancer equal in impact to Big Business—nothing could be more distorted, even granting a sizeable union bureaucracy. But in addition to public exagerations, the labor crisis can be measured in several ways. First, the high expectations of the newborn AFL-CIO of 30 million members by 1965 are suffering a reverse unimaginable five years ago. The demise of the dream of "organizing the unorganized" is dramatically reflected in the AFL-CIO decision, just two years after its creation, to slash its organizing staff in half. From 15 million members when the AFL and CIO merged, the total has slipped to 13.5 million. During the post-war generation, union membership nationally has increased by 4 million—but the total number of workers has jumped by 13 million. Today only 40 percent of all non-agricultural workers are protected by any form of organization. Second, organizing conditions are going to worsen. Where labor now is strongest—in industries—automation is leading to an attrition of available work. As the number of jobs dwindles, so does labor's power of bargaining, since management can handle a strike in an automated plant more easily than the older mass-operated ones.

More important, perhaps, the American economy has changed radically in the last decade, as suddenly the number of workers producing goods became fewer than the number in "nonproductive" areas—government, trade, finance, services, utilities, transportation. Since World War II "white collar" and "service" jobs have grown twice as fast as have "blue collar" production jobs. Labor has almost no organization in the expanding occupational areas of the new economy, but almost all of its entrenched strength in contracting areas. As big government hires more, as business seeks more office workers and skilled technicians, and as growing commercial America demands new hotels, service stations and the like, the conditions will become graver still. Further, there is continuing hostility to labor by the Southern states and their industrial interests—meaning "runaway" plants, cheap labor threatening the organized trade union movement, and opposition from Dixiecrats to favorable labor legislation in Congress. Finally, there is indication that Big Business, for the sake of public relations if nothing more, has acknowledged labor's "right" to exist, but has deliberately tried to contain labor at its present strength, preventing strong unions from helping weaker ones or from spreading to unorganized sectors of the economy. Business is aided in its efforts by proliferation of "right-to-work" laws at state levels (especially in areas where labor is without organizing strength to begin with), and anti-labor legislation in Congress.

In the midst of these besetting crises, labor itself faces its own problems of vision and program. Historically, there can be no doubt as to its worth in American politics—what progress there has been in meeting human needs in this century rests greatly with the labor movement. And to a considerable extent the social democracy for which labor has fought externally is reflected in its own essentially democratic character: representing millions of people, not millions of dollars; demanding their welfare, not eternal profit.

Today labor remains the most liberal "mainstream" institution —but often its liberalism represents vestigial commitments, self-interestedness, unradicalism. In some measure labor has succumbed to institutionalization, its social idealism waning under the tendencies of bureaucracy, materialism, business ethics. The successes of the last generation perhaps have braked, rather than accelerated, labor's zeal for change. Even the House of Labor has bay windows: not only is this true of the labor elites, but as well of some of the rank-and-file. Many of the latter are indifferent unionists, uninterested in meetings, alienated from the complexities of the labor-management negotiating apparatus, lulled to comfort by the accessibility of luxury and the opportunity of long-term contracts. "Union democracy" is not simply inhibited by labor-leader elitism, but by the related problem of rank-and-file apathy to the tradition of unionism. The crisis of labor is reflected in the coexistence within the unions of militant Negro discontents and discriminatory locals, sweeping critics of the obscuring "public interest" marginal tinkering of government and willing handmaidens of conservative political leadership, austere sacrifiers and business-like operators, visionaries and anachronisms—tensions between extremes that keep alive the possibilities for a more militant unionism. Too there are seeds of rebirth in the "organizational crisis" itself: the technologically unemployed, the unorganized white collar men and women, the migrants and farm workers, the unprotected Negroes, the poor, all of whom are isolated now from the power structure of the economy, but who are the potential base for a broader and more forceful unionism.

HORIZON. In summary: a more reformed, more human capitalism, functioning at three-fourths capacity while one-third of America and two-thirds of the world goes needy, domination of politics and the economy by fantastically rich elites, accommodation and limited effectiveness by the labor movement, hardcore poverty and unemployment, automation confirming the dark ascension of machine over man instead of shared abundance, technological change being introduced into the economy by the criteria of profitability—this has been our inheritance. However inadequate, it has instilled quiescence in liberal hearts—partly reflecting the extent to which misery has been overcome, but also the eclipse of social ideals. Though many of us are "affluent," poverty, waste, elitism, manipulation are too manifest to go unnoticed, too clearly unnecessary to go accepted. To change the Cold War status quo and other social evils, concern with the challenges to the American economic machine must expand. Now, as a truly better social state becomes visible, a new poverty impends: a poverty of vision, and a poverty of political action to make that vision reality. Without new vision, the failure to achieve our potentialities will spell the inability of our society to endure in a world of obvious, crying needs and rapid change.

THE INDIVIDUAL IN
THE WARFARE STATE

BUSINESS AND POLITICS, WHEN SIGNIFICANTLY MILITARIZED, affect the whole living condition of each American citizen. Worker and family depend on the Cold War for life. Half of all research and development is concentrated on military ends. The press mimics conventional cold war opinion in its editorials. In less than a full generation, most Americans accept the military-industrial structure as "the way things are." War is still pictured as one kind of diplomacy, perhaps a gloriously satisfying kind. Our saturation and atomic bombings of Germany and Japan are little more than memories of past "policy necessities" that proceeded the wonderful economic boom of 1946. The facts that our once-revolutionary 20,000-ton Hiroshima Bomb is now paled by 50 megaton weapons, that our lifetime has included the creation of intercontinental ballistic missiles, that "greater" weapons are to follow, that weapons refinement is more rapid than the development of weapons of defense, that soon a dozen or more nations will have the Bomb, that one simple miscalculation could incinerate mankind: these orienting facts are but remotely felt. A shell of moral callous separates the citizen from sensitivity to the common peril: this is the result of a lifetime saturation with horror. After all, some ask, where could we begin, even if we wanted to? After all, others declare, we can only assume things are in the best of hands. A coed at the University of Kentucky says, "we regard peace and war as fairy tales." And a child has asked in helplessness, perhaps for us all, "Daddy, why is there a cold war?"

Past senselessness permits present brutality; present brutality is prelude to future deeds of still greater inhumanity; that is the moral history of the twentieth century, from the First World War to the present. A half-century of accelerating destruction has flattened out the individual's ability to make moral distinction; it has made people understandably give up; it has forced private worry and public silence.

To a decisive extent, the means of defense, the military technology itself, determines the political and social character of the state being defended—that is, defense mechanisms themselves in the nuclear age alter the character of the system that creates them for protection. So it has been with America, as her democratic institutions and habits have shriveled in almost direct proportion to the growth of her armaments. Decisions about military strategy, including the monstrous decision to go to war, are more and more the property of the military and industrial arms race machine, with the politicians assuming a ratifying role instead of a determining one. This is increasingly a fact not just because of the installation of the permanent military, but because of constant revolutions in military technology. The new technologies allegedly require military expertise, scientific comprehension, and the mantle of secrecy. As Congress relies more and more on the Joint Chiefs of Staff, the existing chasm between people and decision-makers becomes irreconcilably wide, and more alienating in its effects.

A necessary part of the military effort is propaganda: to "sell" the need for congressional appropriations, to conceal various business scandals, and to convince the American people that the arms race is important enough to sacrifice civil liberties and social welfare. So confusion prevails about the national needs, while the three major services and the industrial allies jockey for power—the Air Force tending to support bombers and missilery; the Navy, Polaris and carriers; the Army, conventional ground forces and invulnerable nuclear arsenals, and all three feigning unity by support of the policy of weapons and agglomeration called the "mix." Strategies are advocated on the basis of power and profit, usually more so than on the basis of national military needs. In the meantime, Congressional investigating committees—most notably the House Un-American Activities Committee and the Senate Judiciary Committee— attempt to curb the little dissent that finds it way into off-beat magazines. A huge militant anti-communist brigade throws in its support, patriotically willing to do *anything* to achieve "total victory" in the Cold War; the government advocates peaceful confrontation with international Communism, then utterly pillories and outlaws the tiny American Communist Party. University professors withdraw prudently from public issues; the very style of social science writing becomes more qualified. Needs in housing, education, minority rights, health care, land redevelopment, hourly wages, all are subordinated—though a political tear is shed gratuitously—to the primary objective of the "military and economic strength of the Free World."

What are the governing policies which supposedly justify all this human sacrifice and waste? With few exceptions they have reflected the quandries and confusion, stagnation and anxiety, of a stalemated nation in a turbulent world. They have shown a slowness, sometimes a sheer inability to react to a sequence of new problems.

Of these problems, two of the newest are foremost: the existence of poised nuclear weapons and the revolutions against the former colonial powers. In both areas, the Soviet Union and the various national communist movements have aggravated international relations in inhuman and undesirable ways, but hardly so much as to blame only communism for the present menacing situation.

DETERRENCE POLICY

THE ACCUMULATION OF NUCLEAR ARSENALS, THE THREAT OF accidental war, the possibility of limited war becoming illimitable holocaust, the impossibility of achieving final arms superiority or invulnerability, the approaching nativity of a cluster of infant atomic powers; all of these events are tending to undermine traditional concepts of power relations among nations. War can no longer be considered as an effective instrument of foreign policy, a means of strengthening alliances, adjusting the balance of power, maintaining national sovereignty, or preserving human values. War is no longer simply a forceful extension of foreign policy; it can obtain no constructive ends in the modern world. Soviet or American "megatonnage" is sufficient to destroy all existing social structures as well as value systems. Missiles have (figuratively) thumbed their nosecones at national boundaries. But America, like other countries, still operates by means of national defense and deterrence systems. These are seen to be useful so long as they are never fully used: unless we as a national entity can convince Russia that we are willing to commit the most heinous action in human history, we will be forced to commit it.

Deterrence advocates, all of them prepared at least to threaten mass extermination, advance arguments of several kinds. At one pole are the minority of open partisans of preventive war—who falsely assume the inevitability of violent conflict and assert the lunatic efficacy of striking the first blow, assuming that it will be easier to "recover" after thermonuclear war than to recover now from the grip of the Cold War. Somewhat more reluctant to advocate initiating a war, but perhaps more disturbing for their numbers within the Kennedy administration, are the many advocates of the "counterforce" theory of aiming strategic nuclear weapons at military installations—though this might "save" more lives than a preventive war, it would require drastic, provacative and perhaps impossible social change to separate many cities from weapon sites, it would be impossible to insure the immunity of cities after one or two counterforce nuclear "exchanges," it would generate a perpetual arms race for less vulnerability and greater weapons power and mobility, it would make outer space a region subject to militarization, and accelerate the suspicions and arms buildups which are incentives to precipitate nuclear action.

Others would support fighting "limited wars" which use conventional (all but atomic) weapons, backed by deterrents so mighty that both sides would fear to use them—although underestimating the implications of numerous new atomic powers on the world stage, the extreme difficulty of anchoring international order with weapons of only transient invulnerability, the potential tendency for a "losing side" to push limited protracted fighting on the soil of underdeveloped countries. Still other deterrence artists propose limited, clearly defensive and retaliatory, nuclear capacity, always potent enough to deter an opponent's aggressive designs—the best of deterrence strategems, but inadequate when it rests on the equation of an arms "stalemate" with international stability.

All the deterrence theories suffer in several common ways. They allow insufficient attention to preserving, extending, and enriching democratic values, such matters being subordinate rather than governing in the process of conducting foreign policy. Second, they inadequately realize the inherent instabilities of the continuing arms race and balance of fear. Third, they operationally tend to eclipse interest and action toward disarmament by solidifying economic, political, and even moral investments in continuation of tensions. Forth, they offer a disinterested and even patriotic rationale for the boondoogling, belligerence, and privilege of military and economic elites. Finally, deterrence strategems invariably understate or dismisse the relatedness of various dangers; they inevitably lend tolerability to the idea of war by neglecting the dynamic interaction of problems—such as the menace of accidental war, the probable future tensions surrounding the emergence of ex-colonial nations, the imminence of several new nations joining the "Nuclear Club," the destabilizing potential of technological breakthrough by either arms race contestant, the threat of Chinese atomic might, the fact that "recovery" after World War III would involve not only human survivors but, as well, a huge and fragile social structure and culture which would be decimated perhaps irreparably by total war.

Such a harsh critique of what we are doing as a nation by no means implies that sole blame for the Cold War rests on the United States. Both sides have behaved irresponsibly—the Russians by an exaggerated lack of trust, and by much dependence on aggressive military strategists rather than on proponents of nonviolent conflict and coexistence. But we do contend, as Americans concerned with the conduct of our representative institutions, that our government has blamed the Cold War stalemate on nearly everything but its own hesitations, its own anachronistic dependence on weapons. To be sure, there is more to disarmament than wishing for it. There are inadequacies in international rule-making institutions—which could be corrected. There are faulty inspection mechanisms—which could be perfected by disinterested scientists. There are Russian intransigency and evasiveness—which do not erase the fact that the Soviet Union, because of a strained economy, an expectant population, fears of Chinese potential, and interest in the colonial revolution, is increasingly disposed to real disarmament with real controls. But there is, too, our own reluctance to face the uncertain world beyond the Cold War, our own shocking assumption that the risks of the present are fewer than the risks of a policy re-orientation to disarmament, our own unwillingness to face the implementation of our rhetorical commitments to peace and freedom.

Today the world alternatively drifts and plunges toward a terrible war—when vision and change are required, our government pursues a policy of macabre dead-end dimensions— conditioned, but not justified, by actions of the Soviet bloc.

Ironically, the war which seems so close will not be fought between the United States and Russia, not externally between two national entities, but as an international civil war throughout the unrespected and unprotected *civitas* which spans the world.

THE COLONIAL
REVOLUTION

WHILE WEAPONS HAVE ACCELERATED MAN'S OPPORTUNITY FOR self-destruction, the counter-impulse to life and creation is superbly manifest in the revolutionary feelings of many Asian, African and Latin American peoples. Against the individual initiative and aspiration, and social sense of organicism characteristic of these upsurges, the American apathy and stalemate stand in embarrassing contrast.

It is difficult today to give human meaning to the welter of facts that surrounds us. That is why it is especially hard to understand the facts of "underdevelopment": in India, man and beast together produced 65 percent of the nation's economic energy in a recent year, and of the remaining 35 percent of inanimately produced power almost three fourths was obtained by burning dung. But in the United States, human and animal power together account for only 1 percent of the national economic energy—that is what stands humanly

97

behind the vague term "industrialization." Even to maintain the misery of Asia today at a constant level will require a rate of growth tripling the national income and the aggregate production in Asian countries by the end of the century. For Asians to have the (unacceptable) 1950 standard of Europeans, less than $2,000 per year for a family, national production must increase 21-fold by the end of the century, and that monstrous feat only to reach a level that Europeans find intolerable.

What has America done? During the years 1955–57 our total expenditures in economic aid were equal to one-tenth of one percent of our total Gross National Product. Prior to that time it was less; since then it has been a fraction higher. Immediate social and economic development is needed—we have helped little, seeming to prefer to create a growing gap between "have" and "have not" rather than to usher in social revolutions which would threaten our investors and our military alliances. The new nations want to avoid power entanglements that will open their countries to foreign domination—and we have often demanded loyalty oaths. They do not see the relevance of uncontrolled free enterprise in societies without accumulated capital and a significant middle class—and we have looked caluminously on those who would not try "our way." They seek empathy—and we have sided with the old colonialists, who now are trying to take credit for "giving" all the freedom that has been wrested from them, or we "empathize" when pressure absolutely demands it.

With rare variation, American foreign policy in the fifties was guided by a concern for foreign investment and a negative anti-communist political stance linked to a series of military alliances, both undergirded by military threat. We participated unilaterally—usually through the Central Intelligence Agency—in revolutions against governments in Laos, Guatemala, Cuba, Egypt, Iran. We permitted economic investment to decisively affect our foreign policy: sugar in Cuba, oil in the Middle East, diamonds and gold in South Africa (with whom we trade more than with any African nation). More exactly: America's "foreign market" in the late fifties, including exports of goods and services plus overseas sales by American firms, averaged about 60 billion annually. This represented twice the investment of 1950, and it is predicted that the same rates of increase will continue. The reason is obvious; *Fortune* said in 1958, "foreign earnings will more than double in ten years, more than twice the probable gain in domestic profits." These investments are concentrated primarily in the Middle East and Latin America, neither region being an impressive candidate for the long-run stability, political caution, and lower-class tolerance that American investors typically demand.

Our pugnacious anti-communism and protection of interests has led us to an alliance inappropriately called the "Free World." It includes four major parliamentary democracies: ourselves, Canada, Great Britain, and India. It also has included through the years Batista, Franco, Verwoerd, Salazar, De Gaulle, Boun Oum, Ngo Diem, Chiang Kai Shek, Trujillo, the Somozas, Saud, Ydigoras—all of these non-democrats separating us deeply from the colonial revolutions.

Since the Kennedy administration began, the American government seems to have initiated policy changes in the colonial and underdeveloped areas. It accepted "neutralism" as a tolerable principle; it sided more than once with the Angolans in the United Nations; it invited Souvanna Phouma to return to Laos after having overthrown his neutralist government there; it implemented the Alliance for Progress that President Eisenhower proposed when Latin America appeared on the verge of socialist revolutions; it made derogatory statements about the Trujillos; it cautiously suggested that a democratic socialist government in British Guina might be necessary to support; in inaugural oratory, it suggested that a moral imperative was involved in sharing the world's resources with those who have been previously dominated. These were hardly sufficient to heal the scars of past activity and present associations, but nevertheless they were motions away from the fifties. But quite unexpectedly, the President ordered the Cuban invasion, and while the American press railed about how we had been "shamed" and defied by that "monster Castro," the colonial peoples of the world wondered whether our foreign policy had really changed from its old imperialist ways (we had never supported Castro, even on the eve of his taking power, and had announced early that "the conduct of the Castro government toward foreign private enterprise in Cuba" would be a main State Department concern). Any heralded changes in our foreign policy are now further suspect in the wake of the Punta Del Este foreign ministers' conference where the five countries representing most of Latin America refused to cooperate in our plans to further "isolate" the Castro government.

Ever since the colonial revolution began, American policy makers have reacted to new problems with old "gunboat" remedies, often thinly disguised. The feeble but desirable efforts of the Kennedy administration to be more flexible are coming perhaps too late, and are of too little significance to really change the historical thrust of our policies. The hunger problem is increasing rapidly mostly as a result of the world-wide population explosion that cancels out the meager triumphs gained so far over starvation. The threat of population to economic growth is simply documented: in 1960–70 population in Africa south of the Sahara will increase 14 percent; in South Asia and the Far East by 22 percent; in North Africa 26 percent; in the Middle East by 27 percent; in Latin America 29 percent. Population explosion, no matter how devastating, is neutral. But how long will it take to create a relation of trust between America and the newly-developing societies? How long to change our policies? And what length of time do we have?

The world is in transformation, but America is not. It can race to industrialize the world, tolerating occasional authoritarianisms, socialisms, neutralisms along the way—or it can slow the pace of the inevitable and default to the eager and self-interested Soviets and, much more importantly, to mankind itself. Only mystics would guess we have opted thoroughly for the first. Consider what our people think of this, the most urgent issue on the human agenda. Fed by a bellicose press, manipulated by economic and political opponents of change, drifting in their own history, they grumble about "the foreign aid waste," or about "that beatnik down in Cuba," or how "things will get us by" . . . thinking confidently, albeit in the usual bewilderment, that Americans can go right on as always, 5 percent of mankind producing 40 percent of its goods.

ANTI-COMMUNISM

AN UNREASONING ANTI-COMMUNISM HAS BECOME A MAJOR social problem for those who want to construct a more democratic America. McCarthyism and other forms of exaggerated and conservative anti-communism seriously weaken democratic institutions and spawn movements contrary to the interests of basic freedoms and peace. In such an atmosphere even the most intelligent of Americans fear to join political organizations, sign petitions, speak out on serious issues. Militaristic policies are easily "sold" to a public fearful of a demonic enemy. Political debate is restricted, thought standardized, action inhibited by the demands of "unity" and "oneness" in the face of the declared danger. Even many liberals and socialists share static and repetitious participation in the anti-communist crusade and often discourage tentative, inquiring discussion about "the Russian question" within their ranks—often by employing "stalinist," "stalinoid," "trotskyite," and other epithets in an oversimplifying way to discredit opposition.

Thus much of the American anti-communism takes on the characteristic of paranoia. Not only does it lead to the perversion of democracy and to the political stagnation of a warfare society, but it also has the unintended consequence of preventing an honest and effective approach to the issues. Such an approach would require public analysis and debate of world politics. But almost nowhere in politics is such a rational analysis possible to make.

It would seem reasonable to expect that in America the basic issues of the Cold War should be rationally and fully debated, between persons of every opinion—on television, on platforms, and through other media. It would seem, too, that there should be a way for a person or an organization to oppose communism *without* contributing to the common fear of associations and public actions. But these things do not happen; instead, there is finger-pointing and comical debate about the most serious of issues. This trend of events on the domestic scene, toward greater irrationality on major questions, moves us to greater concern than does the "internal threat" of domestic communism. Democracy, we are convinced, requires every effort to set in peaceful opposition the basic viewpoints of the day; only by conscious, determined, though difficult, efforts in this direction will the issue of communism be met appropriately.

The government called out the Chicago police, the National Guard, and even U.S. combat troops from Vietnam to protect the 1968 Chicago Democratic Convention. Photos by Paul Sequeria.

Above: Chicago 1968. The war and repression killed the hopes of Port Huron. Dr. Martin Luther King's last dream, to form a united poor people's campaign, died with him. Dr. King's organization nonetheless sent a mule train to Chicago, as they had promised to, in solidarity with the 1968 protests. Photo courtesy of Michael Ochs Archives.

Right: Fannie Lou Hamer, a share-cropper from Ruleville, Mississippi, and a leader of the Mississippi Freedom Democrats. She spoke at a SDS northern community organizing workshop, designed to build the national movement, on the weekend that Malcolm X was killed in 1965.

With Newark Community Union Project activists Anita Warren, left, and Terry Jefferson. Organizing in the slums of the North was meant to complement the southern movement and generate the national focus on poverty and racism envisioned at Port Huron. Photo courtesy of the State Historical Society of Wisconsin.

SNCC leaders Bob Moses (standing), Bob Zellner (left), and James Forman. They exemplified the emphasis on direct action and participatory democracy, and organized the Mississippi Freedom Democratic Party. Photo by Norris McNamara, SNCC, Atlanta, Georgia. Mary Elizabeth King Collection. Courtesy of the State Historical Society of Wisconsin.

Right: As a senior at the University of Michigan and editor of the campus paper, 1961. Photo courtesy of *Mademoiselle* magazine, Condé Nast Publications.

Below: The war on poverty was eclipsed by the Vietnam War, which had been mentioned only in passing in the *Port Huron Statement.* Interviewing peasants in North Vietnam, December 1965.

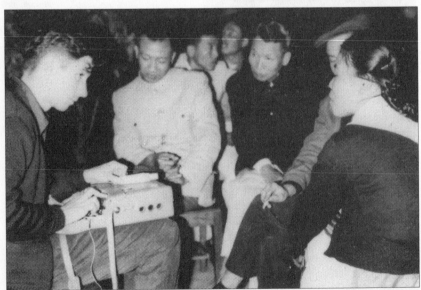

Above: The earliest group portrait of SDS, taken in September of 1963. From left to right: myself, Don McKelvey, Jon Seldin, Nada Chandler, Nancy Hollander, Steve Max, Danny Millstone, Vernon Grizzard, Paul Booth, Carl Wittman, Mary McGroarty, Steve Johnson, Sarah Murphy, Lee Webb, Todd Gitlin, Dick Flacks, Mickey Flacks, Robb Burlage, Rennie Davis. Photo by George Abbot White.

Above: Sharon Jeffrey, a founding member of SDS in Ann Arbor. Her mother, Mildred Jeffrey, a United Auto Workers official, arranged the UAW retreat center in Port Huron as the site of the 1962 conference.

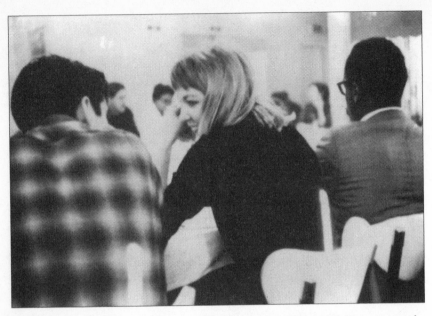

Above: Sandra Cason (Casey), a leader of campus sit-ins in Austin, Texas, 1960. We were married from 1961 to 1963.

Above: Frank Joyce and me circa 1962.

Richard and Mickey Flacks, their son C. Wright Flacks, and Mickey's mother Sonia. The Flacks came to Port Huron carrying dissatisfactions with the Old Left culture in which they were raised. Dick was my closest collaborator in drafting the *Statement*.

Paul Potter at Oberlin College, an early SDS president and keynote speaker at the first national anti-Vietnam protest, 1965. Photo by C. Clark Kissinger.

Robert Alan Haber, founder of Students for a Democratic Society, Ann Arbor, circa 1960. He was both a big thinker and the glue that held the early SDS together.

Above: Bob Ross, an SDS founder, at a 1963 Ann Arbor rally. Courtesy of Michiganensian Yearbook.

Top right: Dorothy Dawson Burlage and Robb Burlage, both Texans. Dorothy was an early leader in the civil rights movement across the South, and a roommate of Casey Hayden's. Robb was the editor of the *Daily Texan*, who rewrote the economics section of the *Port Huron Statement* ("brother Hayden's draft as amended by brother Karl Marx," he laughed).

Bottom right: In September 1961, I was beaten up in McComb, Mississippi, and ordered out of the state by the Mississippi Sovereignty Commission, along with my friend Paul Potter. This moment was three months before I began the draft of the *Port Huron Statement*.

Top left: During the Chicago trial, 1969. *Top right*: Cesar E. Chavez and myself in the 1970s. The United Farm Workers and Chavez appeared three years after Port Huron as a voice of the poor, similar to, but more lasting than, the early SNCC and SDS organizing campaigns. *Bottom*: Myself, Reverend Jesse Jackson, and American Indian Movement leader Dennis Banks in the early '70s. Jackson, an outsider in '68, became a Democratic Party delegate, replacing Mayor Richard Daley in 1972, and later a presidential candidate.

Top: Student Nonviolent Coordinating Committee founders Charles McDew and John Lewis, here at a fortieth reunion, were inspirational and instrumental in the formation of SDS. *Bottom:* Michael Vester, right, a German exchange student at Bowdoin College in 1962, represented the German socialist youth organization also known as SDS at Port Huron. He played an important role in drafting the sections on the Cold War, anticipating the later radical student and anti-missile movements in West Germany. Now a retired professor in Frankfurt, he and I met again at a University of Heidelberg conference on the German and American SDS in 2005. Photo by Martin Klimke.

COMMUNISM AND FOREIGN POLICY

AS DEMOCRATS WE ARE IN BASIC OPPOSITION TO THE COMMUNIST system. The Soviet Union, as a system, rests on the total suppression of organized opposition, as well as a vision of the future in the name of which much human life has been sacrificed, and numerous small and large denials of human dignity rationalized. The Communist Party has equated falsely the "triumph of true socialism" with centralized bureaucracy. The Soviet state lacks independent labor organizations and other liberties we consider basic. And despite certain reforms, the system remains almost totally divorced from the image officially promulgated by the Party. Communist parties throughout the rest of the world are generally undemocratic in internal structure and mode of action. Moreover, in most cases they have subordinated radical programs to requirements of Soviet foreign policy. The communist movement has failed, in every sense, to achieve its stated intentions of leading a worldwide movement for human emancipation.

But present trends in American anti-communism are not sufficient for the creation of appropriate policies with which to relate to and counter communist movements in the world. In no instance is this better illustrated than in our basic national policy-making assumption that the Soviet Union is inherently expansionist and aggressive, prepared to dominate the rest of the world by military means. On this assumption rests the monstrous American structure of military "preparedness"; because of it we sacrifice values and social programs to the alleged needs of military power.

But the assumption itself is certainly open to question and debate. To be sure, the Soviet state has used force and the threat of force to promote or defend its perceived national interests. But the typical American response has been to equate the use of force—which in many cases might be dispassionately interpreted as a conservative, albeit brutal, action—with the initiation of a worldwide military onslaught. In addition, the Russian-Chinese conflicts and the emergence of rifts throughout the communist movement call for a re-evaluation of any monolithic interpretations. And the apparent Soviet disinterest in building a first-strike arsenal of weapons challenges the weight given to protection against surprise attack in formulations of American policy toward the Soviet.

Almost without regard to one's conception of the dynamics of Soviet society and foreign policy, it is evident that the American military response has been more effective in deterring the growth of democracy than communism. Moreover, our prevailing policies make difficult the encouragement of skepticism, anti-war or pro-democratic attitudes in the communist systems. America has done a great deal to foment the easier, opposite tendency in Russia: suspicion, suppression, and stiff military resistance. We have established a system of military alliances which are of even dubious deterrence value. It is reasonable to suggest that "Berlin" and "Laos" have become earth-shaking situations partly because rival systems of deterrence make impossible the withdrawal of threats. The "status quo" is not cemented by mutual threat but by mutual fear of receding from pugnacity—since the latter course would undermine the "credibility" of our deterring system. Simultaneously, while billions in military aid were propping up right wing Laotian, Formosan, Iranian, and other regimes, American leadership never developed a purely political policy for offering concrete alternatives to either communism or the status quo for colonial revolutions. The results have been: fulfillment of the communist belief that capitalism is stagnant, its only defense being dangerous military adventurism; destabilizing incidents in numerous developing countries; an image of America allied with corrupt oligarchies counterposed to the Russian-Chinese image of rapid, though brutal, economic development. Again and again, America mistakes the static area of defense, rather than the dynamic area of development, as the master need of two-thirds of mankind.

Our paranoia about the Soviet Union has made us incapable of achieving agreements absolutely necessary for disarmament and the preservation of peace. We are hardly able to see the possibility that the Soviet Union, though not "peace-loving," may be seriously interested in disarmament.

Infinite possibilities for both tragedy and progress lie before us. On the one hand, we can continue to be afraid, and out of fear commit suicide. On the other hand, we can develop a fresh and creative approach to world problems which will help to create democracy at home and establish conditions for its growth elsewhere in the world.

DISCRIMINATION

OUR AMERICA IS STILL WHITE.

Consider the plight, statistically, of its greatest nonconformists, the "nonwhite" (a Census Bureau designation).

LITERACY: One out of every four "nonwhites" is functionally illiterate; half do not complete elementary school; one in five finishes high school or better. But one in twenty whites is functionally illiterate; four of five finish elementary school; half go through high school or better.

SALARY: In 1959 a "nonwhite" worker could expect to average $2,844 annually; a "nonwhite" family, including a college-educated father, could expect to make $5,654 collectively. But a white worker could expect to make $4,487 if he worked alone; with a college degree and a family of helpers he could expect $7,373. The approximate

Negro-white wage ratio has remained nearly level for generations, with the exception of the World War II employment "boom" which opened many better jobs to exploited groups.

WORK: More than half of all "nonwhites" work at laboring or service jobs, including one-fourth of those with college degrees; one in 20 works in a professional or managerial capacity. Fewer than one in five of all whites are laboring or service workers, including one in every 100 of the college-educated; one in four is in professional or managerial work.

UNEMPLOYMENT: Within the 1960 labor force of approximately 72 million, one of every 10 "nonwhites" was unemployed. Only one of every 20 whites suffered that condition.

HOUSING: The census classifies 57 percent of all "nonwhite" houses substandard, but only 27 percent of white-owned units so exist.

EDUCATION: More than 50 percent of America's "nonwhite" high school students never graduate. The vocational and professional spread of curriculum categories offered "nonwhites" is 16 as opposed to the 41 occupations offered to the white student. Furthermore, in spite of the 1954 Supreme Court decision, of all "nonwhites" educated, 80 percent are educated actually, or virtually, under segregated conditions. And only one of 20 "nonwhite" students goes to college as opposed to the 1:10 ratio for white students.

VOTING: While the white community is registered above two-thirds of its potential, the "nonwhite" population is registered below one-third of its capacity (with even greater distortion in areas of the Deep South).

Even against this background some will say that progress is being made. The facts belie it, however, unless it is assumed that America has another century to deal with its racial inequalities. Others, more pompous, will blame the situation on "those people's inability to pick themselves up," not understanding the automatic way in which such a system can frustrate reform efforts and diminish the aspirations of the oppressed. The one-party system in the South, attached to the Dixiecrat-Republican complex nationally, cuts off the Negro's independent powers as a citizen. Discrimination in employment, along with labor's accommodation to the "lily-white" hiring practices, guarantees the lowest slot in the economic order to the "nonwhite." North or South, these oppressed are conditioned by their inheritance and their surroundings to expect more of the same: in housing, schools, recreation, travel, all their potential is circumscribed, thwarted, and often extinguished. Automation grinds up job opportunities, and ineffective or nonexistent retraining programs make the already-handicapped "nonwhite" even less equipped to participate in "technological progress."

Horatio-Alger Americans typically believe that the "nonwhites" are being "accepted" and "rising" gradually. They see more Negroes on television and so assume that Negroes are "better off." They hear the President talking about Negroes and so assume they are politically represented.

They are aware of black peoples in the United Nations and so assume that the world is generally moving toward integration. They don't drive through the South, or through the slum areas of the big cities, so they assume that squalor and naked exploitation are disappearing. They express generalities about "time and gradualism" to hide the fact that they don't know what is happening.

The advancement of the Negro and other "nonwhites" in America has not been altogether by means of the crusades of liberalism, but rather through unavoidable changes in social structure. The economic pressures of World War II opened new jobs, new mobility, new insights to Southern Negroes, who then began great migrations from the South to the bigger urban areas of the North where their *absolute* wage was greater, though unchanged in relation to the white man of the same stratum. More important than the World War II openings was the colonial revolution. The worldwide upsurge of dark peoples against white colonial domination stirred the aspiration and created an urgency among American Negroes, while simultaneously it threatened the power structure of the United States enough to produce concessions to the Negro. Produced by outer pressure from the newly-moving peoples rather than by the internal conscience of the federal government, the gains were keyed to improving the American "image" more than to reconstructing the society that prospered on top of its minorities. Thus the historic Supreme Court decision of 1954, theoretically desegregating Southern schools, was more a proclamation than a harbinger of social change—and is reflected as such in the fraction of Southern school districts which have desegregated, with federal officials doing little to spur the process.

It has been said that the Kennedy administration did more in two years than the Eisenhower administration did in eight. Of this there can be no doubt. But it is analogous to comparing whispers to silence when positively stentorian tones are demanded. President Kennedy lept ahead of the Eisenhower record when he made his second reference to the racial problem; Eisenhower did not utter a meaningful public statement until his last month in office when he mentioned the "blemish" of bigotry.

To avoid conflict with the Dixiecrat-Republican alliance, President Kennedy has developed a civil rights philosophy of "enforcement, not enactment," implying that existing statuatory tools are sufficient to change the lot of the Negro. So far he has employed executive power usefully to appoint Negroes to various offices, and seems interested in seeing the Southern Negro registered to vote. On the other hand, he has appointed at least four segregationist judges in areas where voter registration is a desperate need. Only two civil rights bills, one to abolish the poll tax in five states and another to prevent unfair use of literacy tests in registration, have been proposed—the President giving active support to neither. But even this legislation, lethargically supported, then defeated, was intended to extend only to federal elections. More important, the Kennedy interest in voter registration has not been supplemented with interest in giving the Southern Negro the economic protection that only trade unions can provide.

It seems evident that the President is attempting to win the Negro permanently to the Democratic Party without basically disturbing the reactionary one-party oligarchy in the South. Moreover, the administration is decidely "cool" (a phrase of Robert Kennedy) toward mass nonviolent movements in the South, though, by the support of racist Dixiecrats the administration makes impossible gradual action through conventional channels. The Federal Bureau of Investigation in the South is composed of Southerners and their intervention in situations of racial tension is always after the incident, not before. Kennedy has refused to "enforce" the legal prerogative to keep federal marshals active in Southern areas before, during, and after any "situations" (this would invite Negroes to exercise their rights and it would infuriate the Southerners in Congress because of its "insulting" features).

While corrupt politicians, together with business interests happy with the absence of organized labor in Southern states and with the profits that result from paying the Negro half a "white wage," stymie and slow fundamental progress, it remains to be appreciated that the ultimate wages of discrimination are paid by individuals and not by the state. Indeed the other sides of the economic, political, and sociological coins of racism represent their more profound implications in the private lives, liberties, and pursuits of happiness of the citizen. While hungry nonwhites the world around assume rightful dominance, the majority of Americans fight to keep integrated housing out of the suburbs. While a fully interracial world becomes a biological probability, most Americans persist in opposing marriage between the races.

While cultures generally interpenetrate, white America is ignorant still of nonwhite America — and perhaps glad of it. The white lives almost completely within his immediate, close-up world where things are tolerable, where there are no Negroes except on the bus corner going to and from work, and where it is important that daughter marry right. White, like might, makes right in America today. Not knowing the "nonwhite," however, the white knows something less of himself. Not comfortable around "different people," he reclines in whiteness instead of preparing for diversity. Refusing to yield objective social freedoms to the "nonwhite," the white loses his personal subjective freedom by turning away "from all these damn causes."

White American ethnocentrism at home and abroad reflects most sharply the self-deprivation suffered by the majority of our country which effectively makes it an isolated minority in the world community of culture and fellowship. The awe inspired by the pervasiveness of racism in American life is only matched by the marvel of its historican span in American traditions. The national heritage of racial discrimination via slavery has been a part of America since Christopher Columbus' advent on the new continent. As such, racism not only antedates the Republic and the thirteen colonies, but even the use of the English language in this hemisphere. And it is well that we keep this as a background when trying to understand why racism stands as such a steadfast pillar in the culture and custom of the country. Racial-xenophobia is reflected in the admission of various racial stocks to the country. From the nineteenth century Oriental Exclusion Acts to the most recent updating of the Walter-McCarran Immigration Acts, the nation has shown a continuous contemptuous regard for "nonwhite." More recently, the tragedies of Hiroshima and Korematsu, and our cooperation with Western Europe in the United Nations add treatment to the thoroughness of racist overtones in national life. But the right to refuse service to anyone is no longer reserved to the Americans. The minority groups, internationally, are changing places.

WHAT IS NEEDED?

How to end the Cold War? How to increase democracy in America? These are the decisive issues confronting liberal and socialist forces today. To us, the issues are intimately related, the struggle for one invariably being a struggle for the other. What policy and structural alternatives are needed to obtain these ends?

1. *Universal controlled disarmament must replace deterrence and arms control as the national defense goal.*

The strategy of mutual threat can only temporarily prevent thermonuclear war, and it cannot but erode democratic institutions here while consolidating oppressive institutions in the Soviet Union. Yet American leadership, while giving rhetorical due to the ideal of disarmament, persists in accepting mixed deterrence as its policy formula: under Kennedy we have seen first-strike and second-strike weapons, countermilitary and counterpopulation inventions, tactical atomic weapons and guerilla warriors, etc. The convenient rationalization that our weapons *potpourri* will confuse the enemy into fear of misbehaving is absurd and threatening. Our own intentions, once clearly retaliatory, are now ambiguous since the President has indicated we might in certain circumstances be the first to use nuclear weapons. We can expect that Russia will become more anxious herself, and perhaps even prepare to "preempt" us, and we (expecting the worst from the Russians) will nervously consider "pre-emption" ourselves. The symmetry of threat and counterthreat leads not to stability but to the edge of hell.

It is necessary that America make disarmament, not nuclear deterrence, "credible" to the Soviets and to the world. That is, disarmament should be continually avowed as a national goal; concrete plans should be presented at conference tables; real machinery for a disarming and disarmed world—national and international—should be created while the disarming process itself goes on. The long-standing idea of unilateral initiative should be implemented as a basic feature of American disarmament strategy: initiatives that are graduated in their risk potential, accompanied by invitations to reciprocation, done regardless of reciprocation, openly planned for a significant period of future time. Their functions should not be to strip America of weapons, but to induce a climate in which disarmament can be discussed with less mutual hostility and threat. They might include: a unilateral nuclear test moratorium, withdrawal of several bases near the Soviet Union, proposals to experiment in disarmament by stabilization of zone of controversy; cessation of all apparent first-strike preparations, such as the development of 41 Polaris submarines by 1963 while naval theorists state that about 45 constitute a provocative force; inviting a special United Nations agency to observe and inspect the launchings of all American flights into outer space; and numerous others.

There is no simple formula for the content of an actual disarmament treaty. It should be phased: perhaps on a region-by-region basis, the conventional weapons first. It should be conclusive, non-open-ended, in its projection. It should be controlled: national inspection systems are adequate at first, but should be soon replaced by international devices and teams. It should be more than denuding: world or at least regional enforcement agencies, an international civil service and inspection service, and other supranational groups must come into reality under the United Nations.

2. *Disarmament should be seen as a political issue, not a technical problem.*

Should this year's Geneva negotiations have resulted (by magic) in a disarmament agreement, the United States Senate would have refused to ratify it, a domestic depression would have begun instantly, and every fiber of American life would be wrenched drastically: these are indications not only of our unpreparedness for disarmament, but also that disarmament is not "just another policy shift." Disarmament means a deliberate shift in most of our domestic and foreign policy.

A. It will involve major changes in economic direction. Government intervention in new areas, government regulation of certain industrial price and investment practices to prevent inflation, full use of national productive capacities, and employment for every person in a dramatically expanding economy all are to be expected as the "price" of peace.

B. It will involve the simultaneous creation of international rule-making and enforcement machinery beginning under the United Nations, and the gradual transfer of sovereignties—such as national armies and national determination of "international" law—to such machinery.

C. It will involve the initiation of an explicitly political—as opposed to military—foreign policy on the part of the two major superstates. Neither has formulated the political terms in which they would conduct their behavior in a disarming or disarmed world. Neither dares to disarm until such an understanding is reached.

3. *A crucial feature of this political understanding must be the acceptance of status quo possessions.*

According to the universality principle all present national entities—including the Vietnams, the Koreas, the Chinas, and the Germanys—should be members of the United Nations as sovereign, no matter how desirable, states.

Russia cannot be expected to negotiate disarmament treaties for the Chinese. We should not feed Chinese fanaticism with our encirclement but Chinese stomachs with the aim of making war contrary to Chinese policy interests. Every day that we support anti-communist tyrants but refuse to even allow the Chinese Communists representation in the United Nations marks a greater separation of our ideals and our actions, and it makes more likely bitter future relations with the Chinese.

Second, we should recognize that an authoritarian Germany's insistence on reunification, while knowing the impossibility of achieving it with peaceful means, could only generate increasing frustrations among the population and nationalist sentiments which frighten its Eastern neighbors who have historical reasons to suspect Germanic intentions. President Kennedy himself told the editor of *Izvestia* that he fears an independent Germany with nuclear arms, but American policies have not demonstrated cognizance of the fact that Chancellor Adenauer too, is interested in continued East-West tensions over the Germany and Berlin problems and nuclear arms precisely because this is the rationale for extending his domestic power and his influence upon the NATO-Common Market alliance.

A world war over Berlin would be absurd. Anyone concurring with such a proposition should demand that the West cease its contradictory advocacy of "reunification of Germany through free elections" and "a rearmed Germany in NATO." It is a dangerous illusion to assume that Russia will hand over East Germany to a rearmed reunited Germany which will enter the Western camp, although this Germany might have a Social Democratic majority which could prevent a reassertion of German nationalism. We have to recognize that the cold war and the incorporation of Germany into the two power blocs was a decision of both Moscow and Washington, of both

Adenauer and Ulbricht. The immediate responsibility for the Berlin Wall is Ulbricht's. But it had to be expected that a regime which was bad enough to make people flee is also bad enough to prevent them from fleeing. The inhumanity of the Berlin wall is an ironic symbol of the irrationality of the cold war, which keeps Adenauer and Ulbricht in power. A reduction of the tension over Berlin, if by internationalization or by a recognition of the status quo and reducing provocations, is a necessary but equally temporary measure which could not ultimately reduce the basic cold war tension to which Berlin owes its precarious situation. The Berlin problem cannot be solved without reducing tensions in Europe, possibly by a bilateral military disengagement and creating a neutralized buffer zone. Even if Washington and Moscow were in favor of disengagement, both Adenauer and Ulbricht would never agree to it because cold war keeps their parties in power.

Until their regimes' departure from the scene of history, the Berlin status quo will have to be maintained while minimizing the tensions necessarily arising from it. Russia cannot expect the United States to tolerate its capture by the Ulbricht regime, but neither can America expect to be in a position to indefinitely use Berlin as a fortress within the communist world. As a fair and bilateral disengagement in Central Europe seems to be impossible for the time being, a mutual recognition of the Berlin status quo, that is, of West Berlin's and East Germany's security, is needed. And it seems to be possible, although the totalitarian regime of East Germany and the authoritarian leadership of West Germany until now succeeded in frustrating all attempts to minimize the dangerous tensions of cold war.

The strategy of securing the status quo of the two power

blocs until it is possible to depolarize the world by creating neutralist regions in all trouble zones seems to be the only way to guarantee peace at this time.

4. Experiments in disengagement and demilitarization must be conducted as part of the total disarming process.

These "disarmament experiments" can be of several kinds, so long as they are consistent with the principles of containing the arms race and isolating specific sectors of the world from the Cold War power-play. First, it is imperative that no more nations be supplied with, or locally produce, nuclear weapons. A 1959 report of the National Academy of Arts and Sciences predicted that 19 nations would be so armed in the near future. Should this prediction be fulfilled, the prospects of war would be unimaginably expanded. For this reason the United States, Great Britain, and the Soviet Union should band against France (which wants its own independent deterrent) and seek, through United Nations or other machinery, the effective prevention of the spread of atomic weapons. This would involve not only declarations of "denuclearization" in whole areas of Latin America, Africa, Asia, and Europe, but would attempt to create inspection machinery to guarantee the peaceful use of atomic energy.

Second, the United States should reconsider its increasingly outmoded European defense framework, the North Atlantic Treaty Organization. Since its creation in 1949, NATO has assumed increased strength in overall determination of Western military policy, but has become less and less revelant to its original purpose, which was the defense of Central

Europe. To be sure, after the Czech coup of 1948, it might have appeared that the Soviet Union was on the verge of a full-scale assault on Europe. But that onslaught has not materialized, not so much because of NATO's existence but because of the general unimportance of much of Central Europe to the Soviets. Today, when even American-based ICBM's could smash Russia minutes after an invasion of Europe, when the Soviets have no reason to embark on such an invasion, and when "thaw sectors' are desperately needed to brake the arms race, one of the least threatening but most promising courses for America would be toward the gradual diminishment of the NATO force, coupled with the negotiated "disengagement" of parts of Central Europe.

It is especially crucial that this be done while America is entering into favorable trade relations with the European Economic Community: such a gesture, combining economic ambition with less dependence on the military, would demonstrate the kind of competitive "coexistence" America intends to conduct with the communist-bloc nations. If the disengaged states were the two Germanies, Poland, and Czechoslovakia, several other benefits would accrue. First, the United States would be breaking with the lip-service commitment of "liberation" of Eastern Europe which has contributed so much to Russian fears and intransigence, while doing too little about actual liberation. But the end of "liberation" as a proposed policy would *not* signal the end of American concern for the oppressed in Eastern Europe. On the contrary, disengagement would be a real, rather than a rhetorical, effort to ease military tensions, thus undermining the Russian argument for tighter controls in Eastern Europe based on the "menace of capitalist encirclement." This policy, geared to the needs of democratic elements in the satellites, would develop a real bridge between East and West across the two most pro-Western Russian satellites. The Russians in the past have indicated some interest in such a plan, including the demilitarization of the Warsaw pact countries. Their interest should be publicly tested. If disengagement could be achieved, a major zone could be removed from the Cold War, the German problem would be materially diminished, and the need for NATO would diminish, and attitudes favorable to disarming would be generated.

Needless to say, these proposals are much different than what is currently being practiced and praised. American military strategists are slowly acceding to the NATO demand for an independent deterrent, based on the fear that America might not defend Europe from military attack. These tendencies strike just the opposite chords in Russia than those which would be struck by disengagement themes: the chords of military alertness, based on the fact that NATO (bulwarked by the German Wehrmacht) is preparing to attack Eastern Europe or the Soviet Union. Thus the alarm which underlies the NATO proposal for an independent deterrent is likely itself to bring into existence the very Russian posture that was the original cause of fear. Armaments spiral and belligerence will carry the day, not disengagement and negotiation.

THE INDUSTRIALIZATION OF THE WORLD

MANY AMERICANS ARE PRONE TO THINK OF THE INDUSTRI-
alization of the newly-developed countries as a modern form
of American noblesse, undertaken sacrificially for the benefit of others. On the contrary, the task of world industrialization, of eliminating the disparity between have and
have-not nations, is as important as any issue facing America.
The colonial revolution signals the end of an era for the old
Western powers and a time of new beginnings for most of the
people of the earth. In the course of these upheavals, many
problems will emerge: American policies must be revised or
accelerated in several ways.

1. *The United States' principal goal should be creating
a world where hunger, poverty, disease, ignorance, violence, and exploitation are replaced as central features by
abundance, reason, love, and international cooperation.*

To many this will seem the product of juvenile hallucination: but we insist it is a more realistic goal than is a world of nuclear stalemate. Some will say this is a hope beyond all bounds: but it is far better to us to have positive vision than a "hard-headed" resignation. Some will sympathize, but claim it is impossible: if so, then, we, not Fate, are the responsible ones, for we have the means at our disposal. *We should not give up the attempt for fear of failure.*

2. We should undertake here and now a fifty-year effort to prepare for all nations the conditions of industrialization.

Even with far more capital and skill than we now import to emerging areas, serious prophets expect that two generations will pass before accelerating industrialism is a worldwide act. The needs are numerous: every nation must build an adequate infrastructure (transportation, communication, land resources, waterways) for future industrial growth; there must be industries suited to the rapid development of differing raw materials and other resources; education must begin on a continuing basis for everyone in the society, especially including engineering and technical training; technical assistance from outside sources must be adequate to meet present and long-term needs; atomic power plants must spring up to make electrical energy available. With America's idle productive capacity, it is possible to begin this process immediately without changing our military allocations. This might catalyze a "peace race" since it would demand a response of such magnitude from the Soviet Union that arms spending and "coexistence" spending would become strenuous, perhaps impossible, for the Soviets to carry on simultaneously.

3. *We should not depend significantly on private enterprise to do the job.*

Many important projects will not be profitable enough to entice the investment of private capital. The total amount required is far beyond the resources of corporate and philanthropic concerns. The new nations are suspicious, legitimately, of foreign enterprises dominating their national life. World industrialization is too huge an undertaking to be formulated or carried out by private interests. Foreign economic assistance is a national problem, requiring long range planning, integration with other domestic and foreign policies, and considerable public debate and analysis. Therefore the federal government should have primary responsibility in this area.

4. *We should not lock the development process into the Cold War: we should view it as a way of ending that conflict.*

When President Kennedy declared that we must aid those who need aid because it is right, he was unimpeachably correct—now principle must become practice. We should reverse the trend of aiding corrupt anti-communist regimes. To support dictators like Diem while trying to destroy ones like Castro will only enforce international cynicism about American "principle," and is bound to lead to even more authoritarian revolutions, especially in Latin America where we did not even consider foreign aid until Castro had challeneged the status quo. We should end the distinction between communist hunger and anti-communist hunger. To feed only anti-communists is to directly fatten men men like Boun Oum, to incur the wrath of real democrats and to distort our own sense of human values. We must cease seeing development in terms of communism and capitalism. To fight communism by capitalism in the newly-developing areas is to fundamentally misunderstand the international hatred of imperialism and colonialism and to confuse the needs of 19th century industrial America with those of contemporary nations.

Quite fortunately, we are edging away from the Dullesian "either-or" foreign policy ultimatum toward an uneasy acceptance of neutralism and nonalignment. If we really desire the end of the Cold War, we should now welcome nonalignment—that is, the creation of whole blocs of nations concerned with growth and with independently trying to break out of the Cold War apparatus.

Finally, while seeking disarmament as the genuine deterrent, we should shift from financial support of military regimes to support of national development. Real security cannot be gained by propping up military defenses, but only through the hastening of political stability, economic growth, greater social welfare, improved education. Military aid is temporary in nature, a "shoring up" measure that only postpones crisis. In addition, it tends to divert the allocations of the nation being defended to supplementary military spending (Pakistan's budget is 70 percent oriented to defense measures). Sometimes it actually creates crisis situations, as in Latin America where we have contributed to the growth of national armies which are opposed generally to sweeping democratization. Finally, if we are really generous, it is harder for corrupt governments to exploit unfairly economic aid—especially if it is so plentiful that rulers cannot blame the absence of real reforms on anything but their own power lusts.

5. *America should show its commitment to democratic institutions not by withdrawing support from undemocratic regimes, but by making domestic democracy exemplary.*

Worldwide amusement, cynicism, and hatred toward the United States as a democracy is not simply a communist propaganda trick, but an objectively justifiable phenomenon. If respect for democracy is to be international, then the significance of democracy must emanate from American shores, not from the "soft sell" of the United States Information Agency.

6. *America should agree that public utilities, railroads, mines, and plantations, and other basic economic institutions should be in the control of national, not foreign, agencies.*

The destiny of any country should be determined by it nationals, not by outsiders with economic interests within. We should encourage our investors to turn over their foreign holdings (or at least 50 percent of the stock) to the national governments of the countries involved.

7. Foreign aid should be given through international agencies, primarily the United Nations.

The need is to eliminate political overtones, to the extent possible, from economic development. The use of international agencies, with interests transcending those of American or Russian self-interest, is the feasible means of working on sound development. Second, internationalization will allow more long-range planning, integrate development plans adjacent countries and regions may have, and eliminate the duplication built into national systems of foreign aid. Third, it would justify more strictness of supervision than is now the case with American foreign aid efforts, but with far less chance of suspicion on the part of the developing countries. Fourth, the humiliating "hand-out" effect would be replaced by the joint participation of all nations in the general development of the earth's resources and industrial capacities. Fifth, it would eliminate national tensions, e.g. between Japan and some Southeast Asian areas, which now impair aid programs by "disguising" nationalities in the common pooling of funds. Sixth, it would make easier the task of stabilizing the world market prices of basic commodities, alleviating the enormous threat that decline in prices of commodity exports might cancel out the gains from foreign aid in the new nations. Seventh, it would improve the possibilities of non-exploitative development, especially in creating "soft-credit" rotating-fund agencies which would not require immediate progress or financial return. Finally, it would enhance the importance of the United Nations itself, as the disarming process would enhance the UN as a rule-enforcement agency.

8. *Democratic theory must confront the problems inherent in social revolutions.*

For Americans concerned with the development of democratic societies, the anti-colonial movements and revolutions in the emerging nations pose serious problems. We need to face the problems with humility: after 180 years of constitutional government we are still striving for democracy in our own society. We must acknowledge that democracy and freedom do not magically occur, but have roots in historical experience; they cannot always be demanded for any society at any time, but must be nurtured and facilitated. We must avoid the arbitrary projection of Anglo-Saxon democratic forms onto different cultures. Instead of democratic capitalisms we should anticipate more or less authoritarian variants of socialism and collectivism in many emergent societies.

But we do not abandon our critical faculties. Insofar as these regimes represent a genuine realization of national independence, and are engaged in constructing social systems which allow for personal meaning and purpose where exploitation once was, economic systems which work for the people where once they oppressed them, and political systems which allow for the organization and expression of minority opinion and dissent, we recognize their revolutionary and positive character. Americans can contribute to the growth of democracy in such societies not by moralizing, nor by indiscriminate prejudgment, but by retaining a critical identification with these nations, and by helping them to avoid external threats to their independence. Together with students and radicals in these nations we need to develop a reasonable theory of democracy which is concretely applicable to the cultures and conditions of hungry people.

TOWARD AMERICAN
DEMOCRACY

EVERY EFFORT TO END THE COLD WAR AND EXPAND THE
process of world industrialization is an effort hostile to people
and institutions whose interests lie in perpetuation of the East-
West military threat and the postponement of change in the
"have-not" nations of the world. Every such effort, too, is
bound to establish greater democracy in America. The major
goals of a domestic effort would be:

1. *America must abolish its political party stalemate.*

Two genuine parties, centered around issues and essential
values, demanding allegiance to party principles shall sup-
plant the current system of organized stalemate which is seriously inadequate to a world in flux. It has long been argued
that the very overlapping of American parties guarantees that
issues will be considered responsibly, that progress will be

gradual instead of intemperate, and that therefore America will remain stable instead of torn by class strife. On the contrary: the enormous party overlap itself confuses issues and makes responsible presentation of choice to the electorate impossible, that guarantees Congressional listlessness and the drift of power to military and economic bureaucracies, that directs attention away from the more fundamental causes of social stability, such as a huge middle class, Keynesian economic techniques, and Madison Avenue advertising. The ideals of political democracy, then, the imperative need for flexible decision-making apparatus makes a real two-party system an immediate social necessity. What is desirable is sufficient party disagreement to dramatize major issues, yet sufficient party overlap to guarantee stable transitions from administration to administration.

Every time the President criticizes a recalcitrant Congress, we must ask that he no longer tolerate the Southern conservatives in the Democratic Party. Every time a liberal representative complains that "we can't expect everything at once" we must ask if we received much of anything from Congress in the last generation. Every time he refers to "circumstances beyond control" we must ask why he fraternizes with racist scoundrels. Every time he speaks of the "unpleasantness of personal and party fighting" we should insist that pleasantry with Dixiecrats is inexcusable when the dark peoples of the world call for American support.

2. *Mechanisms of voluntary association must be created through which political information can be imparted and political participation encouraged.*

Political parties, even if realigned, would not provide adequate outlets for popular involvement. Institutions should be created that engage people with issues and express political preference, not as now with huge business lobbies which exercise undemocratic *power*, but which carry political *influence* (appropriate to private, rather than public, groupings) in national decision-making enterprise. Private in nature, these should be organized around single issues (medical care, transportation systems reform, etc.), concrete interest (labor and minority group organizations), multiple issues or general issues. These do not exist in America in quantity today. If they did exist, they would be a significant politicizing and educative force bringing people into touch with public life and affording them means of expression and action. Today, giant lobby representatives of business interests are dominant, but not educative. The federal government itself should counter the latter forces whose intent is often public deceit for private gain, by subsidizing the preparation and decentralized distribution of objective materials on all public issues facing government.

3. *Institutions and practices which stifle dissent should be abolished, and the promotion of peaceful dissent should be actively promoted.*

The First Amendment freedoms of speech, assembly, thought, religion and press should be seen as guarantees, not threats, to national security. While society has the right to prevent active subversion of its laws and institutions, it has the duty as well to promote open discussion of all issues—otherwise it will be in fact promoting real subversion as the only means of implementing ideas. To eliminate the fears and apathy from national life it is necessary that the institutions bred by fear and apathy be rooted out: the House Un-American Activities Committee, the Senate Internal Security Committee, the loyalty oaths on federal loans, the Attorney General's list of subversive organizations, the Smith and McCarran Acts. The process of eliminating the blighting institutions is the process of restoring democratic participation. Their existence is a sign of the decomposition and atrophy of participation.

4. *Corporations must be made publicly responsible.*

It is not possible to believe that true democracy can exist where a minority utterly controls enormous wealth and power. The influence of corporate elites on foreign policy is neither reliable nor democratic; a way must be found to subordinate private American foreign investment to a democratically con-structed foreign policy. The influence of the same giants on domestic life is intolerable as well; a way must be found to direct our economic resources to genuine human needs, not the private needs of corporations nor the rigged needs of maneuvered citizenry.

We can no longer rely on competition of the many to insure that business enterprise is responsive to social needs. The many have become the few. Nor can we trust the corporate bureaucracy to be socially responsible or to develop a "corporate conscience" that is democratic. The community of interest of corporations, the anarchic actions of industrial leaders, should become structurally responsible to the people—and truly to the people rather than to an ill-defined and questionable "national interest." Labor and government as presently constituted are not sufficient to "regulate" corporations. A new reordering, a new calling of responsibility is necessary: more than changing "work rules" we must consider changes in the rules of society by challenging the unchallenged politics of American corporations. Before the government can really begin to control business in a "public interest," the public must gain more substantial control of government: this demands a movement for political as well as economic realignments. We are aware that simple government "regulation," if achieved, would be inadequate without increased worker participation in management decision-making, strengthened and independent regulatory power, balances of partial and/or complete public ownership, various means of humanizing the conditions and types of work itself, sweeping welfare programs and regional *public* development authorities. These are examples of measures to rebalance the economy toward public — and individual — control.

5. *The allocation of resources must be based on social needs. A truly "public sector" must be established, and its nature debated and planned.*

At present the majority of America's "public sector," the largest part of our public spending, is for the military. When great social needs are so pressing, our concept of "government spending" is wrapped up in the "permanent war economy."

In fact, if war is to be avoided, the "permanent war economy" must be seen as an "*interim* war economy." At some point, America must return to other mechanisms of economic growth besides public military spending. We must plan economically in peace. The most likely, and least desirable, return would be in the form of private enterprise. The undesirability lies in the fact of inherent capitalist instability, noticeable even with bolstering effects of government intervention. In the most recent post-war recessions, for example, private expenditures for plant and equipment dropped from $16 billion to $11.5 billion, while unemployment surged to nearly 6 million. By good fortune, investments in construction industries remained level, else an economic depression would have occurred. This will recur, and our growth in national per capita living standards will remain unsensational while the economy stagnates.

The main *private* forces of economic expansion cannot guarantee a steady rate of growth, nor acceptable recovery from recession—especially in a demilitarizing world. Government participation will inevitably expand enormously, because the stable growth of the economy demands increasing "public" investments yearly. Our present outpour of more than $500 billion might double in a generation, irreversibly involving government solutions. And in future recessions, the compensatory fiscal action by the government will be the only means of avoiding the twin disasters of greater unemployment and a slackening rate of growth. Furthermore, a close relationship with the European Common Market will involve competion with numerous planned economies and may aggravate American unemployment unless the economy here is expanding swiftly enough to create new jobs.

All these tendencies suggest that not only solutions to our present social needs but our future expansion rests upon our willingness to enlarge the "public sector" greatly. Unless we choose war as an economic solvent, future public spending will be of non-military nature—a major intervention into civilian production by the government. The issues posed by this development are enormous:

A. How should public vs. private domain be determined? We suggest these criteria: 1) when a resource has been discovered or developed with public tax revenues, such as a space communications system, it should remain a public resource, not be given away to private enterprise; 2) when monopolization seems inevitable, the public should maintain control of an industry; 3) when national objectives contradict seriously with business objectives as to the use of the resource, the public need should prevail.

B. How should technological advances be introduced into a society? By a public process, based on publicly-determined needs. Technological innovations should not be postponed from social use by private corporations in order to protect investment in older equipment.

C. How shall the "public sector" be made public, and not the arena of a ruling bureaucracy of "public servants"? By steadfast opposition to bureaucratic coagulation, and to definitions of human needs according to problems easiest for computers to solve. Second, the bureaucratic pile-ups must be at least minimized by local, regional, and national economic *planning*—

responding to the interconnection of public problems by comprehensive programs. Third, and most important, by experiments in *decentralization*, based on the vision of man as master of his machines and his society. The personal capacity to cope with life has been reduced everywhere by the introduction of technology that only minorities of men (barely) understand. How the process can be reversed—and we believe it can be—is one of the greatest sociological and economic tasks before human people today. Polytechnical schooling, with the individual adjusting to several work and life experiences, is one method. The transfer of certain mechanized tasks back into manual forms, allowing men to make whole, not partial products, is not unimaginable. Our monster cities, based historically on the need for mass labor, might now be humanized, broken into smaller communities, powered by nuclear energy, arranged according to community decision. These are but a fraction of the opportunities of the new era: serious study and deliberate experimentation, rooted in a desire for human fraternity, may now result in blueprints of civic paradise.

6. *America should concentrate on its genuine social priorities: abolish squalor, terminate neglect, and establish an environment for people to live in with dignity and creativeness.*

A. A program against *poverty* must be just as sweeping as the nature of poverty itself. It must not be just palliative, but directed to the abolition of the structural circumstances of poverty. At a bare minimum it should include a housing act far larger than the one supported by the Kennedy administration, but one that is geared more to low-and middle-income needs than to the windfall aspirations of small and large private entrepreneurs, one that is more sympathetic to the quality of communal life than to the efficiency of city-split highways. Second, *medical care* must become recognized as a lifetime human right just as vital as food, shelter, and clothing—the federal government should guarantee health insurance as a basic social service turning medical treatment into a social habit, not just an occasion of crisis, fighting sickness among the aged, not just by making medical care financially feasible but by reducing sickness among children and younger people. Third, existing institutions should be expanded so the Welfare State cares for *everyone's* welfare according to need. *Social Security* payments should be extended to everyone and should be proportionately greater for the poorest. A *minimum wage* of at least $1.50 should be extended to all workers (including the 16 million currently not covered at all). Programs for equal *educational opportunity* are as important a part of the battle against poverty.

B. A full-scale public initiative for civil rights should be undertaken despite the clamor among conservatives (and liberals) about gradualism, property rights, and law and order. The executive and legislative branches of the federal government should work by enforcement *and* enactment against any form of exploitation of minority groups. No federal cooperation with racism is tolerable—from financing of schools, to the development of federally-supported industry, to the social gatherings of the President. Laws hastening school desegregation, voting rights, and economic protection for Negroes are needed right now. The moral force of the Executive Office should be exerted against the Dixiecrats specifically, and the national complacency about the race question generally. Especially in the North, where one half of the country's Negro people now live, civil rights is not a problem to be solved in isolation from other problems. The fight against poverty, against slums, against the stalemated Congress, against McCarthyism, are all fights against the discrimination that is nearly endemic to all areas of American life.

C. The promise and problems of long-range *federal economic development* should be studied more constructively. It is an embarrassing paradox that the Tenessee Valley Authority is a wonder to most foreign visitors but a "radical" and barely influential project to most Americans. The Kennedy decision to permit private facilities to transmit power from the $1 billion Colorado River Storage Project is a disastrous one, interposing privately-owed transmitters between publicly-owned generators and their publicly (and cooperatively) owned distributors. The contrary trend, to public ownership of power, should be generated in an experimental way.

The Area Redevelopment Act of 1961 is a first step in recognizing the underdeveloped areas of the United States. It is only a drop in the bucket financially and is not keyed to public planning and public works on a broad scale. It consists only of a few loan programs to lure industries and some grants to improve public facilities to lure these industries. The current public works bill in Congress is needed—and a more sweeping, higher-priced program of regional development with a proliferation of "TVAs" in such areas as the Apalachian region are needed desperately. However, it has been rejected already by Mississippi because the improvement it bodes for the unskilled Negro worker. This program should be enlarged, given teeth, and pursued rigorously by federal authorities.

D. We must meet the growing complex of "city" problems; over 90 percent of Americans will live in urban areas within two decades. Juvenile delinquency, untended mental illness, crime increase, slums, urban tenantry and non–rent controlled housing, the isolation of the individual in the city—all are problems of the city and are major symptoms of the present system of economic priorities and lack of public planning. Private property control (the real estate lobby and a few selfish landowners and businesses) is as devastating in the cities as corporations are on the national level. But there is no comprehensive way to deal with these problems now amidst competing units of government, dwindling tax resources, suburban escapism (saprophitic to the sick central cities), high infrastructure costs and no one to pay them.

The only solutions are national and regional. "Federalism" has thus far failed here because states are rural-dominated; the federal government has had to operate by bootlegging and trickle-down measures dominated by private interests, with their appendages through annexation or federation. A new external challenge is needed, not just a Department of Urban Affairs but a thorough national *program* to help the cities. The *model* city must be projected—more community decision-making and participation, true integration of classes, races, vocations—provision for beauty, access to nature and the benefits of the central city as well, privacy without privatism, decentralized "units" spread horizontally with central, regional democratic control—provision for the basic facility-needs, for everyone, with units of planned *regions* and thus public, democratic control over the growth of the civic community and the allocation of resources.

E. *Mental health* institutions are in dire need; there were fewer mental hospital *beds* in relation to the numbers of mentally ill in 1959 than there were in 1948. Public hospitals, too, are seriously wanting; existing structures alone need an estimated $1 billion for rehabilitation. Tremendous staff and faculty needs exist as well, and there are not enough medical students enrolled today to meet the anticipated needs of the future.

F. Our *prisons* are too often the enforcers of misery. They must be either re-oriented to rehabilitative work through public supervision or be abolished for their dehumanizing social effects. Funds are needed, too, to make possible a decent prison environment.

G. *Education* is too vital a public problem to be completely entrusted to the province of the various states and local units. In fact, there is no good reason why America should not progress now toward internationalizing rather than localizing, its education system—children and young adults studying everywhere in the world, through a United Nations program, would go far to create mutual understanding. In the meantime, the need for teachers and classrooms in America is fantastic. This is an area where "minimal" requirements should hardly be considered as a goal—there always are improvements to be made in the education system, e.g., smaller classes and many more teachers for them, programs to subsidize the education for the poor but bright, etc.

H. America should eliminate *agricultural policies* based on scarcity and pent-up surplus. In America and foreign countries there exist tremendous needs for more food and balanced diets. The federal government should finance small farmers' cooperatives, strengthen programs of rural electrification, and expand policies for the distribution of agricultural surpluses throughout the world (by Food-for-Peace and related UN programming). Marginal farmers must be helped to either become productive enough to survive "industrialized agriculture" or given help in making the transition out of agriculture—the current Rural Area Development program must be better coordinated with a massive national "area redevelopment" program.

I. *Science* should be employed to constructively transform the conditions of life throughout the United States and the world. Yet at the present time the Department of Health, Education, and Welfare and the National Science Foundation together spend only $300 million annually for scientific purposes in contrast to the $6 billion spent by the Defense Department and the Atomic Energy Commission. One-half of all research and development in America is directly devoted to military purposes. Two imbalances must be corrected—that of military over non-military investigation, and that of biological-natural-physical science over the sciences of human behavior. Our political system must then include planning for the human use of science: by anticipating the political consequences of scientific innovation, by directing the discovery and exploration of space, by adapting science to improved production of food, to international communications systems, to technical problems of disarmament, and so on. For the newly-developing nations, American science should focus on the study of cheap sources of power, housing and building materials, mass educational techniques, etc. Further, science and scholarship should be seen less as an apparatus of conflicting power blocs, but as a bridge toward supra-national community: the International Geophysical Year is a model for continuous further cooperation between the science communities of all nations.

ALTERNATIVES TO HELPLESSNESS

THE GOALS WE HAVE SET ARE NOT REALIZABLE NEXT MONTH, or even next election—but that fact justifies neither giving up altogether nor a determination to work only on immediate, direct, tangible problems. Both responses are a sign of helplessness, tearfulness of visions, refusal to hope, and tend to bring on the very conditions to be avoided. Fearing vision, we justify rhetoric or myopia. Fearing hope, we reinforce despair.

The first effort, then, should be to state a vision: what is the perimeter of human possibility in this epoch? This we have tried to do. The second effort, if we are to be politically responsible, is to evaluate the prospects for obtaining at least a substantial part of that vision in our epoch: what are the social forces that exist, or that must exist, if we are to be at all successful? And what role have we ourselves to play as a social force?

1. In exploring the existing social forces, note must be taken of the Southern civil rights movement as the most heartening beacuse of the justice it insists upon, exemplary because it indicates that there can be a passage out of apathy.

This movement, pushed into a brilliant new phase by the Montgomery bus boycott and the subsequent nonviolent action of the sit-ins and Freedom Rides has had three major results: first, a sense of self-determination has been instilled in millions of oppressed Negroes; second, the movement has challenged a few thousand liberals to new social idealism; third, a series of important concessions have been obtained, such as token school desegregation, increased administration help, new laws, desegregation of some public facilities.

But fundamental social change—that would break the props from under Jim Crow—has not come. Negro employment opportunity, wage levels, housing conditions, educational privileges—these remain deplorable and relatively constant, each deprivation reinforcing the impact of the others. The Southern states, in the meantime, are strengthening the fortresses of the status quo, and are beginning to camouflage the fortresses by guile where open bigotry announced its defiance before. The white-controlled one-party system remains intact; and even where the Republicans are beginning under the pressures of industrialization in the towns and suburbs, to show initiative in fostering a two-party system, all Southern state Republican Committees (save Georgia) have adopted militant segregationist platforms to attract Dixiecrats.

Rural dominance remains a fact in nearly all the Southern

states, although the reapportionment decision of the Supreme Court portends future power shifts to the cities. Southern politicians maintain a continuing aversion to the welfare legislation that would aid their people. The reins of the Southern economy are held by conservative businessmen who view human rights as secondary to property rights. A violent anticommunism is rooting itself in the South, and threatening even moderate voices. Add the militaristic tradition of the South, and its irrational regional mystique and one must conclude that authoritarian and reactionary tendencies are a rising obstacle to the small, voiceless, poor, and isolated democratic movements.

The civil rights struggle thus has come to an impasse. To this impasse, the movement responded this year by entering the sphere of politics, insisting on citizenship rights, specifically the right to vote. The new voter registration stage of protest represents perhaps the first major attempt to exercise the conventional instruments of political democracy in the struggle for racial justice. The vote, if used strategically by the great mass of now-unregistered Negroes theoretically eligible to vote, will be a decisive factor in changing the quality of Southern leadership from low demagoguery to decent statesmanship.

More important, the new emphasis on the vote heralds the use of political means to solve the problems of equality in America, and it signals the decline of the shortsighted view that "discrimination" can be isolated from related social problems. Since the moral clarity of the civil rights movement has not always been accompanied by precise political vision, and sometimes not even by a real political consciousness, the new phase is revolutionary in its implications. The intermediate goal of the program is to secure and insure a healthy respect and realization of Constitutional liberties. This is important not only to terminate the civil and private abuses which currently characterize the region, but also to prevent the pendulum of oppression from simply swinging to an alternate extreme with a new unsophisticated electorate, after the unhappy example of the last Reconstruction. It is the ultimate objectives of the strategy which promise profound change in the politics of the nation. An increased Negro voting rate in and of itself is not going to dislodge racist controls of the Southern power structure; but an accelerating movement through the courts, the ballot boxes, and especially the jails is the most likely means of shattering the crust of political intransigency and creating a semblance of democratic order on local and state levels.

Linked with pressure from Northern liberals to expunge the Dixiecrats from the ranks of the Democratic Party, massive Negro voting in the South could destroy the vice-like grip reactionary Southerners have on the Congressional legislative process.

2. The broadest movement for *peace* in several years emerged in 1961–62. In its political orientation and goals it is much less identifiable than the movement for civil rights: it includes socialists, pacifists, liberals, scholars, militant activists, middle-class women, some professionals, many students, a few unionists. Some have been emotionally single-issue: Ban the Bomb. Some have been academically obscurantist. Some have rejected the System (sometimes both systems). Some have attempted,

also, to "work within" the system. Amidst these conflicting streams of emphasis, however, certain basic qualities appear. The most important is that the "peace movement" has operated almost exclusively through peripheral institutions—almost never through mainstream institutions. Similarly, individuals interested in peace have nonpolitical social roles that cannot be turned to the support of peace activity. Concretely, liberal religious societies, anti-war groups, voluntary associations and ad hoc committees have been the political unit of the peace movement; and its human movers have been students, teachers, housewives, secretaries, lawyers, doctors, clergy. The units have not been located in spots of major social influence; the people have not been able to turn their resources fully to the issues that concern them. The results are political ineffectiveness and personal alienation.

The organizing ability of the peace movement thus is limited to the ability to state and polarize issues. It does not have an institution or a forum in which the conflicting interests can be debated. The debate goes on in corners; it has little connection with the continuing process of determining allocations of resources. This process is not necessarily centralized, however much the peace movement is estranged from it. National policy, though dominated to a large degree by the "power elites" of the corporations and the military, is still partially founded in consensus. It can be altered when there actually begins a shift in the allocation of resources and the listing of priorities by the people in the institutions which have social influence, e.g., the labor unions and the schools. As long as the debates of the peace movement form only a protest, rather than an opposition viewpoint within the centers of serious decision-making, then it is neither a movement of democratic relevance, nor is it likely to have any effectiveness except in educating more outsiders to the issue. It is vital, to be sure, that this educating go on (a heartening sign is the recent proliferation of books and journals dealing with peace and war from newly-developing countries); the possibilities for making politicians responsible to "peace constituencies" becomes greater.

But in the long interim before the national political climate is more open to deliberate, goal-directed debate about peace issues, the dedicated peace "movement" might well prepare a *local base*, especially by establishing civic committees on the techniques of converting from military to peacetime production. To make war and peace *relevant* to the problems of everyday life, by relating it to the backyard (shelters), the baby (fallout), the job (military contracts)—and making a turn toward peace seem desirable on these same terms—is a task the peace movement is just beginning and can profitably continue.

3. Central to any analysis of the potential for change must be an appraisal of *organized labor*. It would be ahistorical to disregard the immense influence of labor in making modern America a decent place in which to live. It would be confused to fail to note labor's presence today as the most liberal of mainstream institutions. But it would be irresponsible not to criticize labor for losing much of the idealism that once made it a driving movement. Those who expected a labor upsurge after the 1955

AFL-CIO merger can only be dismayed that one year later, in the Stevenson-Eisenhower campaign, the AFL-CIO Committee on Political Education was able to obtain solicited one-dollar contributions from only one of every 24 unionists, and prompt only 40 percent of the rank-and-file to vote.

As a political force, labor generally has been unsuccessful in the post-war period of prosperity. It has seen the passage of the Taft-Hartley and Landrum-Griffin laws, and while beginning to receive slightly favorable National Labor Relations Board rulings, it has made little progress against right-to-work laws. Furthermore, it has seen less than adequate action on domestic problems, especially unemployment.

This labor "recession" has been only partly due to anti-labor politicians and corporations. Blame should be laid, too, to labor itself for not mounting an adequate movement. Labor has too often seen itself as elitist, rather than mass-oriented, and as a pressure group rather than as an 18-million-member body making political demands for all America. In the first instance, the labor bureaucracy tends to be cynical toward, or afraid of, rank-and-file involvement in the work of the union. Resolutions passed at conventions are implemented only by high-level machinations, not by mass mobilization of the unionists. Without a significant base, labor's pressure function is materially reduced since it becomes difficult to hold political figures accountable to a movement that cannot muster a vote from a majority of its members.

There are some indications, however, that labor might regain its missing idealism. First, there are signs within the movement: of worker discontent with their economic progress, of collective bargaining, of occasional splits among union leaders on questions such as nuclear testing or other Cold War issues. Second, and more important, are the social forces which prompt these feelings of unrest. Foremost is the permanence of unemployment, and the threat of automation. But important, too, is the growth of unorganized ranks in white-collar fields. Third, there is the tremendous challenge of the Negro movement for support from organized labor: the alienation from and disgust with labor hypocrisy among Negroes ranging from the NAACP to the Black Muslims (crystallized in the formation of the Negro American Labor Council) indicates that labor must move more seriously in its attempts to organize on an interracial basis in the South and in large urban centers. When this task was broached several years ago, "jurisdictional" disputes prevented action. Today, many of these disputes have been settled—and the question of a massive organizing campaign is on the labor agenda again.

These threats and opportunities point to a profound crisis: either labor will continue to decline as a social force, or it must constitute itself as a mass political force demanding not only that society recognize its rights to organize but also a program going beyond desired labor legislation and welfare improvements. Necessarily this latter role will require rank-and-file involvement. It might include greater autonomy and power for political coalitions of the various trade unions in local areas, rather than the more stultifying dominance of the international unions now. It might include reductions in leaders' salaries, or rotation from executive office to shop obligations, as a means of breaking down the hierarchical tendencies which have detached elite from base and made the highest echelons of labor more like businessmen than workers. It would certainly mean an announced independence of the center and Dixiecrat wings of the Democratic Party, and a massive organizing drive, especially in the South to complement the growing Negro political drive there.

A new politics must include a revitalized labor movement: a movement which sees itself, and is regarded by others, as a major leader of the breakthrough to a politics of hope and vision. Labor's role is no less unique or important in the needs of the future than it was in the past; its numbers and potential political strength, its natural interest in the abolition of exploitation, its reach to the grass roots of American society, combine to make it the best candidate for the synthesis of the civil rights, peace, and economic reform movements.

The creation of bridges is made more difficult by the problems left over from the generation of "silence." Middle-class students, still the main actors in the embryonic upsurge, have yet to overcome their ignorance, and even vague hostility, for what they see as "middle-class-labor" bureaucrats. Students must open the campus to labor through publications, action programs, curricula, while labor opens its house to students through internships, requests for aid (on the picket line, with handbills, in the public dialogue), and politics. And the organization of the campus can be a beginning—teachers' unions can be advocated as both socially progressive, and educationally beneficial; university employees can be organized—and thereby an important element in the education of the student radical.

But the new politics is still contained; it struggles below the surface of apathy, awaiting liberation. Few anticipate the break-through and fewer still exhort labor to begin. Labor continues to be the most liberal—and most frustrated institution in mainstream America.

4. Since the Democratic Party sweep in 1958, there have been exaggerated but real efforts to establish a liberal force in Congress, not to balance but to at least voice criticism of the conservative mood. The most notable of these efforts was the Liberal Project begun early in 1959 by Representative Kastenmeier of Wisconsin. The Project was neither disciplined nor very influential but it was concerned at least with confronting basic domestic and foreign problems, in concert with several liberal intellectuals.

In 1960 five members of the Project were defeated at the polls (for reasons other than their membership in the Project). Then followed a "post mortem" publication of *The Liberal Papers*, materials discussed by the Project when it was in existence. Republican leaders called the book "further out than Communism." The New Frontier administration repudiated any connection with the statements. Some former members of the Project even disclaimed their past roles.

A hopeful beginning came to a shameful end. But during the demise of the Project, a new spirit of Democratic Party reform was occurring: in New York City, Ithaca, Massachusetts, Connecticut, Texas, California, and even in Mississippi and Alabama where Negro candidates for Congress challenged racist political power. Some were for peace, some for the liberal side of the New Frontier, some for realignment of the parties— and in most cases they were supported by students. Here and there were stirrings of organized discontent with the political statemate. Americans for Democratic Action and the *New Republic*, pillars of the liberal community, took stands against the President on nuclear testing. A split, extremely slight thus far, developed in organized labor on the same issue. The Rev. Martin Luther King, Jr., preached against the Dixiecrat-Republican coalition across the nation.

5. From 1960 to 1962, the campuses experienced a revival of idealism among an active few. Triggered by the impact of the sit-ins, students began to struggle for integration, civil liberties, student rights, peace, and against the fast-rising right-wing "revolt" as well. The liberal students, too, have felt their urgency thwarted by conventional channels: from student governments to Congressional committees. Out of this alienation from existing channels has come the creation of new ones; the most characteristic forms of liberal-radical student organizations are the dozens of campus political parties, political journals, and peace inarches and demonstrations. In only a few cases have students built bridges to power: an occasional election campaign, the sit-ins, Freedom Rides, and voter registration activities; in some relatively large Northern demonstrations for peace and civil rights, and infrequently, through the United States National Student Association whose notable work has not been focused on political change.

These contemporary social movements—for peace, civil rights, civil liberties, labor—have in common certain values and goals. The fight for peace is one for a stable and racially integrated world; for an end to the inherently volitale exploitation of most of mankind by irresponsible elites, and for freedom of economic, political and cultural organization. The fight for civil rights is also one for social welfare for all Americans; for free speech and the right to protest; for the shield of economic independence and bargaining power; for the reduction of the arms race which takes national attention and resources away from the problems of domestic injustices. Labor's fight for jobs and wages is also one against exploitation of the Negro as a source of cheap labor; for the right of petition and strike; for world industrialization; for the stability of a peacetime economy instead of the instability of a wartime economy; for expansion of the welfare state. The fight for a liberal Congress is a fight for a platform from which these concerns can issue. And the fight for students, for internal democracy in the university, is a fight to gain a forum for the issues.

But these scattered movements have more in common: a need for their concerns to be expressed by a political party responsible to their interests. That they have no political expression, no political channels, can be traced in large measure to the existence of a Democratic Party which tolerates the perverse unity of liberalism and racism, prevents the social change wanted by Negroes, peace protesters, labor unions, students, reform Democrats, and other liberals. Worse, the party stalemate prevents even the raising of controversy—a full Congressional assault on racial discrimination, disengagement in Central Europe, sweeping urban reform, disarmament and inspection, public regulation of major industries; these and other issues are never heard in the body that is supposed to represent the best thoughts and interests of all Americans. An imperative task for these publicly disinherited groups, then, is to demand a Democratic Party responsible to their interests. They must support Southern voter registration and Negro political candidates and demand that Democratic Party liberals do the same (in the last Congress, Dixiecrats split with Northern Democrats on 119 of 300 roll calls, mostly on civil rights, area redevelopment, and foreign aid bills; the breach was much larger than in the previous several sessions). Labor (either independent or Democratic) should be formed to run against big city regimes on such issues as peace, civil rights, and urban needs. Demonstrations should be held at every Congressional or convention seatings of Dixiecrats. A massive publicity and research campaign should be initiated, showing to every housewife, doctor, professor, and worker the damage done to their interests every day a racist occupies a place in the Democratic Party. Where possible, the peace movement should challenge the "peace credentials" of the otherwise-liberals by threatening or actually running candidates against them.

THE UNIVERSITY AND SOCIAL CHANGE

THERE IS PERHAPS LITTLE REASON TO BE OPTIMISTIC ABOUT the above analysis. True, the Dixiecrat-GOP coalition is the weakest point in the dominating complex of corporate, military and political power. But the civil rights, peace, and student movements are too poor and socially slighted, and the labor movement too quiescent, to be counted with enthusiasm. From where else can power and vision be summoned? We believe that the universities are an overlooked seat of influence.

First, the university is located in a permanent position of social influence. Its educational function makes it indispensable and automatically makes it a crucial institution in the formation of social attitudes. Second, in an unbelievably complicated world, it is the central institution for organizing, evaluating, and transmitting knowledge. Third, the extent to which academic resources presently are used to buttress immoral social practice is revealed first, by the extent to which defense contracts make the universities engineers of the arms race. Too, the use of modern social science as a manipulative tool reveals itself in the "human relations" consultants to the modern corporations, who introduce trivial sops to give laborers feelings of "participation" or "belonging," while actually deluding them in order to further exploit their labor. And, of course, the use of motivational research is already infamous as a manipulative aspect of American politics. But these social uses of the universities' resources also demonstrate the unchangeable reliance by men of power on the men and storehouses of knowledge: this makes the university functionally tied to society in new ways, revealing new potentialities, new levers for change. Fourth, the university is the only mainstream institution that is open to participation by individuals of nearly any viewpoint.

These, at least, are facts, no matter how dull the teaching, how paternalistic the rules, how irrelevant the research that goes on. Social relevance, the accessibility to knowledge, and internal openness—these together make the university a potential base and agency in a movement of social change.

1. Any new left in America must be, in large measure, a left with real intellectual skills, committed to deliberativeness, honesty, reflection as working tools. The university permits the political life to be an adjunct to the academic one, and action to be informed by reason.

2. A new left must be distributed in significant social roles throughout the country. The universities are distributed in such a manner.

3. A new left must consist of younger people who matured in the post-war world, and partially be directed to the recruitment of younger people. The university is an obvious beginning point.

4. A new left must include liberals and socialists, the former for their relevance, the latter for their sense of thoroughgoing reforms in the system. The university is a more sensible place than a political party for these two traditions to begin to discuss their differences and look for political synthesis.

5. A new left must start controversy across the land, if national policies and national apathy are to be reversed. The ideal university is a community of controversy, within itself and in its effects on communities beyond.

6. A new left must transform modern complexity into issues that can be understood and felt close-up by every human being. It must give form to the feelings of help-lessness and indifference, so that people may see the political, social, and economic sources of their private troubles and organize to change society. In a time of supposed prosperity, moral complacency, and political manipulation, a new left cannot rely on only aching stomachs to be the engine force of social reform. The case for change, for alternatives that will involve uncomfortable personal efforts, must be argued as never before. The university is a relevant place for all of these activities.

But we need not indulge in illusions: the university system cannot complete a movement of ordinary people making demands for a better life. From its schools and colleges across the nation, a militant left might awaken its allies, and by beginning the process toward peace, civil rights, and labor struggles, reinsert theory and idealism where too often reign confusion and political barter. The power of students and faculty united is not only potential; it has shown its actuality in the South, and in the reform movements of the North.

The bridge to political power, though, will be built through genuine cooperation, locally, nationally, and internationally, between a new left of young people, and an awakening community of allies. In each community we must look within the university and act with confidence that we can be powerful, but we must look outwards to the less exotic but more lasting struggles for justice.

To turn these possibilities into realities will involve national efforts at university reform by an alliance of students and faculty. They must wrest control of the educational process from the administrative bureaucracy. They must make fraternal and functional contact with allies in labor, civil rights, and other liberal forces outside the campus. They must import major public issues into the curriculum — research and teaching on problems of war and peace is an outstanding example. They must make debate and controversy, not dull pedantic cant, the common style for educational life. They must consciously build a base for their assault upon the loci of power.

As students for a democratic society, we are committed to stimulating this kind of social movement, this kind of vision and program in campus and community across the country. If we appear to seek the unattainable, as it has been said, then let it be known that we do so to avoid the unimaginable.

ABOUT THE AUTHOR

TOM HAYDEN, WHO DRAFTED THE PORT HURON STATEMENT in 1962 when he was twenty-one years old, was among the founders of Students for a Democratic Society, a Freedom Rider in the segregated South, a community organizer in the slums of New Jersey, and an opponent of the Vietnam War who was indicted by Richard Nixon. He eventually served in the California Legislature for eighteen years. He currently teaches at Occidental College and writes on the nature of social movements in Los Angeles. He is the author of nine books, including *The Last Gospel of the Earth, The Whole World Was Watching,* and *Irish Hunger.* The *New York Times* cited his 1988 book *Reunion* as one of the best of the year.